irish
facts

Reviews:

AMAZON REVIEWS ARE APPRECIATED!

designerinkbooks@gmail.com

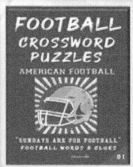  

CONTENTS

chapter one **HISTORY 1**

    PART 1 - IRELAND – IT'S ALL IN THE NAME 2

    PART 2 - HISTORY RULERS OF IRELAND 4

    PART 3 - BLUE, 3 SYMBOLS, FLAG 7

    *PART 4 - PENAL LAWS, CHIEFS, PRESIDENTS &
PRIME MINISTERS 9*

    *PART 5 - RELIGION, PLACES, DUTY FREE,
ACCENTS 11*

    PART 6 - WEATHER 14

    PART 7 - RANDOM FAST FACTS #1 20

chapter two **ST. PATRICK'S DAY, &
PARADES 22**

    PART 1 - LEGEND OF ST. PATRICK 23

    PART 2 - LEPRACHAUNS 26

    PART 3 - ST. PATRICKS DAY CELEBRATIONS 27

    *PART 4 - ST. PATRICKS DAY FOOD, BEER,
FACTS 33*

    PART 5 - FAST FACTS – ST. PATRICK (DAY) 35

chapter three
**EMMIGRATION/IMMIGRATION, BOSTON,
AMERICA, ARGENTINA 38**

    PART 1 - IRISH EVERYWHERE 39

    PART 2 - EMIGRATION TO AMERICA 40

    PART 3 - PORTS OF EMIGRATION 43

    PART 4 - BOSTON IMMIGRANTS 45

    PART 5 - AMERICAN CIVIL WAR 48

    PART 6 - ARGENTINA 51

    PART 7 - RANDOM FAST FACTS #2 52

chapter FOUR **NOTRE DAME 55**

PART 1 - ORIGINS, PEOPLE 56

PART 2 - "FIGHTING IRISH" 58

PART 3 - CAMPUS 61

PART 4 - NOTRE DAME TRADITIONS 64

PART 5 - FAST FACTS -NOTRE DAME 68

chapter Five **NORTHERN IRELAND 70**

PART 1 - WHAT IS NORTHERN IRELAND 71

PART 2 - ORIGINS, OLD NORTHERN IRELAND 73

PART 3 - "THE TROUBLES" 75

PART 4 - TODAY'S NORTHERN IRELAND 77

PART 5 - FAMOUS LANDMARKS AND LOCATIONS 80

PART 6 - FAST FACTS – NORTHERN IRELAND 83

chapter
Six PUBS, ALCOHOL, GUINNESS 87

PART 1 - ALCOHOL CONSUMPTION 88

PART 2 - TOP 10 BEST IRISH BEERS 89

PART 3 - IRISH PUBS "DO'S & DO NOT'S" 91

PART 4 - GUINNESS 93

PART 5 - GUINNESS MUSEUM 95

PART 6 - GUINNESS & NIGERIA 97

PART 7 - FAST FACTS - GUINNESS 98

chapter Seven **DRACULA, MUSIC, FAMOUS PEOPLE 100**

PART 1 - DRACULA 101

PART 2 - MUSIC 102

PART 3 - THE POGUES 103

PART 4 - IRISH DANCING 105

PART 5 - 6 CELEBRITIES NOBODY KNOWS HAVE IRISH ANCESTRY 108

PART 6 - RANDOM FAST FACTS # 3 111

chapter eight TV& MOVIES 114

PART 1 - INDUSTRY, TAX BREAKS 115

PART 2 - BRAVEHEART 116

PART 3 - SAVING PRIVATE RYAN 117

PART 4 - GAME OF THRONES 119

PART 5 - HARRY POTTER AND THE HALF-BLOOD PRINCE 121

PART 6 - THE PRINCESS BRIDE 123

PART 7 - VIKINGS 125

PART 8 - THE TUDORS 127

PART 9 - STAR WARS EPISODE VII: THE FORCE AWAKENS 129

PART 10 - RYAN'S DAUGHTER (1970) 131

PART 11 - RANDOM FAST FACTS #4 133

chapter nine FOOD, TEA, TOBACCO 135

PART 1 - POTATOES 136

PART 2 - STEW & VEGETABLE SOUP 139

PART 3 - FISH 140

PART 4 - BREAD AS POPULAR AS POTATOES 141

PART 5 - TEA 142

PART 6 - TOBACCO 144

PART 7 - RANDOM FAST FACTS #5 145

chapter ten – **LANGUAGE, SLANG, JOKES 147**

PART 1 - GAELIC 148

PART 2 - ENGLISH WORDS INTO IRISH 149

PART 3 - COUNTY SLANG 152

PART 4 - IRISH JOKES 157

PART 5 - IRELAND SLANG 161

PART 6 – RANDOM FAST FACTS #6 162

chapter eleven **SPORTS 164**

PART 1 - SPORTS 165

PART 2 - GAELIC GAMES 166

PART 3 - GAELIC FOOTBALL 167

PART 4 - HURLING 168

PART 5 - BOXING / COMBAT SPORTS 169

PART 6 - FOOTBALL (SOCCER) 170

PART 7 - GOLF 173

PART 8 - RUGBY 174

PART 9 - CRICKET 176

PART 10 - RANDOM FAST FACTS #7 177

chapter twelve **ATHLETES 179**

PART 1 - ROY KEAN - FOOTBALL (SOCCER) MIDFIELDER (B. 1971) 180

PART 2 - LIAM BRADY – FOOTBALL (SOCCER) MIDFIELDER (B. 1956) 181

PART 3 - NICHOLAS CHRISTOPHER MICHAEL "CHRISTY" RING - HURLER (1920-1979) 183

PART 4 - RORY MCILROY, GOLFER, MBE (B. 1989) 184

PART 5 - WILLIAM JOSEPH DUNLOP, OBE, MOTORCYCLIST (1895-1965) 187

PART 6 - PETER CANAVAN - GAELIC FOOTBALLER & MANAGER (B. 1971) 189

PART 7 - ALEX HIGGINS - SNOOKER (1949 - 2010) 191

PART 8 - BRIAN O'DRISCOLL, RUGBY (B. 1979) 193

PART 9 - ROBERT (ROBBIE) KEANE - FORMER FOOTBALL FORWARD (B. 1980) 196

PART 10 - CONOR MCGREGOR - 3 WEIGHT CLASS MMA FIGHTER AND BOXER (B. 1988) 198

PART 11 - RANDOM FAST FACTS #8 203

PART 12 - CREDITS 205

chapter one
HISTORY

PART 1 -
IRELAND – IT'S ALL IN THE NAME

NORSEMAN
According to the oldest known documentation, the Norsemen from Scandinavia dubbed the land "Inis na Fidbadh," which roughly translates to "Isle of the Woods" and alluded to Ireland as the "Westland isle."

A LOT OF LAND
Other theories say that the island was known as the "Abundant Land" by the Proto-Celts, while the Greeks and Romans named Ireland Ierna and/or Hibernia, the last of which is still used by some organizations and groups today!

IRISH GODDESS
The old Irish word "Éiru," which was believed to be an Irish Goddess and the maternal Goddess of the land and sovereignty, is said to have given rise to Éire and, therefore, Ireland.

Chapter One - HISTORY

This connection is quite possible, given Ireland's strong pagan and religious ties over the centuries, but a connection, and mash-up, of all the identities, seems the most likely.

REPUBLIC OR NOT?

The country is still typically called Éire or Ireland today. The term "Republic of Ireland" is occasionally used to distinguish between sporting teams, but it is uncommon.

"ÉIRE" OR "IRELAND"

Since Eamon de Valera's 1937 passage of the Irish Constitution, the contemporary titles of "Éire" or "Ireland" have been in use. Since then, Éire has appeared on a variety of items, including currency, Irish Euros, postal stamps, passport seals, and the President of Ireland's seal.

EMERALD GREEN

The country is also known as the "Emerald Isle," which refers to the lush greenery that covers much of the scenery and countryside.

PART 2 - HISTORY RULERS OF IRELAND

ANCIENT IRELAND

Evidence suggests that the earliest human presence in Ireland dates back to around 12,500 BC. This is later than other parts of Europe owing to the fact that it's an island on the western edge of the continent, and it takes time to get to places.

NEWGRANGE IS 5,000 YEARS OLD.

Newgrange is an outstanding example of a monument known to archaeologists as a passage-grave or passage-tomb in Ireland and Western Europe.

According to the most solid Carbon 14 dates known from archaeology, it was built in approximately 3200BC, which means it is more than 600 years older than Egypt's Giza Pyramids & 1,000 years older than Stonehenge.

As well as being older than the ancient pyramid of Giza and Stonehenge, this ancient burial tomb gets 19 minutes of daylight penetrating through it during the winter solstice.

Chapter One - HISTORY

1100S – 1500S, MILORD

1171-1542 is marked as the Lordship of Ireland age

1542 - 1800 is the Kingdom of Ireland age

1801 - 1922 is the United Kingdom & Ireland age

NO KING, BUT MANY KINGS

The island of Ireland was never unified under a single ruler until the British invaded in 1169 and declared the Island their own. Instead, hundreds of lesser kings were continually at war with one another on an almost permanent basis. This Anglo-Norman invasion of Ireland in 1169 marked the start of British dominance in Ireland.

1500S-1600S

A time of Britain's 400–500-year struggle for complete power. In the 1100's England was considered the noble power in Ireland; however, their rule was not complete, with much of the nation not recognizing the colonizer. The Tudor Conquest, which spanned the 16th and 17th centuries, saw England gradually consolidate its grip on the region by means of increasingly violent means.

THE 1600S

throughout the 1600s, a system of anti-Catholic regulations known as the penal laws were established to disadvantage the Catholic majority and Protestant dissenters in a variety of cruel and unjust ways.

Chapter One - HISTORY

At various points in time the various periods, Catholics were barred from voting, holding public office, serving in the Irish Army, and from entering legal teaching professions.

Intermarriage with Protestants was banned, and any children of the mixed marriage were always brought up in the Protestant faith.

Catholics weren't even allowed to own horses worth over five pounds.

1800S POTATO FAMINE

The Irish potato famine of the 1840s and '50s was one of the most devastating eras in Irish history. All but a small portion of Ireland's potato crop was rendered inedible by disease. As a result, Ireland's population dropped by nearly two (some say three) million people,  primarily due to starvation and mass emigration to the United States.

Nearly 200 years later, Ireland's population has yet to fully recover from the effects of the potato famine. Approximately 8 million people lived in Ireland at that time, which is more than a million more than the 6.6M living on the island today (NI included).

IRELAND – NORTHERN IRELAND - UK

Since 1923 Ireland has been a separate sovereign Nation while Northern Ireland is still under the UK banner.

PART 3 - BLUE, 3 SYMBOLS, FLAG

IT IS OFFICIAL, AZURE BLUE

Historically, azure blue has served as Ireland's official color. This shade of blue has been associated with Saint Patrick since the 1780s when it was chosen as the Anglo-Irish Order of St Patrick's official color.

IRELAND GOES GREEN

As the Irish independence movement gained momentum in the early 1800s, the idea that the British also wore blue became a growing source of contention. The solution? Ireland's rich green countryside supplied the inspiration.

As a result of the quest for sovereignty, Green became famous as the color most associated with Ireland starting in the early nineteenth century.

3 SYMBOLS OF IRELAND

Celtic Cross - Represents knowledge, strength, and compassion.

Harp - represents Irelands' national sovereignty, and is Ireland's official national symbol.

Green Shamrock - Unofficial national flower. St. Patrick inspired symbol for explaining the Holy Trinity to nonbelievers.

Chapter One - HISTORY

IRELAND'S NATIONAL ICON

Contrary to popular belief, the Celtic Harp, not the Shamrock, is the national symbol of Ireland. This means the Emerald Isle is the only country in the world with a musical instrument as its national icon.

FLAG COLORS

Green, white, and orange are the colors of the Irish Tricolour.

GREEN - stands for Catholics, Irish nationalists, Gaelic culture, and an Irish revolution, and it is based on the old green Irish flag with a golden harp on it.

WHITE - is the color of peace, hope, and harmony between Catholics & Protestants; All of the things that the country hoped to accomplish during a period of revolution and transformation.

ORANGE represents Ireland's Protestant minority and is inspired by King William III of England, Scotland, and Ireland AKA "William of Orange."

The design of these three colors in the exact order is to symbolize Ireland's hopeful reunification as a whole.

FLAG RULES

The Irish Tricolour may now be seen flying across all of Ireland's counties.

There are no formal flag laws other than that the green must be nearest to the flagpole, that no other flag shall fly above the Tricolour, and that every effort should be made to elevate it off the ground and away from trees and other obstructions.

PART 4 - PENAL LAWS, CHIEFS, PRESIDENTS & PRIME MINISTERS

PENAL LAWS

Throughout the 17th Century, a set of anti-Catholic rules or penal laws were enacted in order to disadvantage the Catholic majority and Protestant dissenters in a range of unfair and unjust ways.

There were a number of instances in which Catholics had been prohibited from voting, serving in the Irish Army, or even teaching law.

Many periods of time saw intermarriage of Catholics with Protestants discouraged and downright outlawed. And those children of any mixed Catholic-Protestant faiths were to always be brought up Protestant.

Catholics were even barred from owning horses that were worth more than £5.

TEE-SHOOK

The Prime Minister, elected by the Irish Parliament and appointed by the President, also goes by the Irish term "Taoisearch."

Proper Phonetical spelling is "Tee-shakh."

Phonetically speaking, Cambridge Dictionary recommends pronunciation as a 2-syllable beat(s) of "TEE" & "SHOOK" for "TEE-shook"

Secondary sources recommend "Tay" "Shick" for "TAY-shick"

Chapter One - HISTORY

IS IRELAND RULED BY A CHIEF?

Ireland's Prime Minister, or head of government in the Dail, and is referred to in Irish as "Taoisearch."

While the word "Taoiserch" is sometimes equated to a "Chieftain," the proper term is referred to as simply "Chief." This term is gender-neutral, so formally addressing male or female PMs is the same.

PRESIDENT VS. PRIME MINISTER

Both the President and the Prime Minister serve the people within the Dail, Ireland's House of Oireachtas, The National Parliament.

The President (Uachtarn na hireann - in Irish) of Ireland is elected by the people and, much like the USA, serves as the supreme commander of the Irish Defence Forces.

The President also has constitutional responsibilities such as signing parliamentary bills into law and exercising the right to refuse legislation inconsistent with the constitution.

This official represents the Executive arm of government - Ministries in charge of the police and civil service comprise the executive branch. Laws are proposed by the government, then passed by the Senate, signed into law by the president, and implemented by the Taoisearch & party's executive branch.

PART 5 - RELIGION, PLACES, DUTY FREE, ACCENTS

ROMAN CATHOLIC

In Ireland, 88% of the population is officially Roman Catholic. In the Western World, the Republic of Ireland boasts one of the highest percentages of church attendance, with an estimated 45% attending mass regularly.

PROTESTANT

Just 5% of Ireland identifies as Protestant (not including Northern Ireland). Protestantism was on the decline in the 20th century due in large part to the exit of the British military in the early 1900s and the Vatican's law that mixed Catholic-Protestant marriages raise all offspring as Catholic. There has been an uptick of the Protestant following in the 21st century.

DUBLIN'S BEVERLY HILLS

Dalkey, meaning "thorn island" is a Dublin suburb known as Ireland's "Beverly Hills" and is home to many Irish celebrities. This affluent city and seaside resort located SE of Dublin was at one time a Viking settlement and the active port through which the plague of the 1500s came into Ireland.

Chapter One - HISTORY

Famous people like U2's Bono and Edge, George Bernard Shaw, Van Morrison, Enya, James Joyce, and Damon Hill have called it home.

DUTY-FREE, AN IRELAND FIRST
Surprisingly, the first tax-free outlets opened at Shannon Airport in Ireland in 1947.

Brendan O'Regan, Airport Catering Comptroller, persuaded the Irish government to adopt a statute in 1947 declaring Shannon Airport's transit area to be officially outside of Ireland and so exempt from taxation. All of this was a radical idea at the time. But, eventually, the Customs-Free Airport Act passed on March 18, 1947, designated Shannon Airport as the world's first duty-free port.

NEW ACCENT EVERY 10 MILES
It is said there's 1000 accents in the UK, and 900 are Irish. This may be true.

LONGEST NAME
Muckanaghederdauhaulia, translated from Irish to English, is "pig-marsh between two sea inlets" is Ireland's longest place name. It is a mid-northern, west coast 470-acre townland in County Galway, Ireland, in the civil parish of Kilcummin.

NATIONAL LEPRECHAUN MUSEUM
Dublin is home to the World's first and only known museum for leprechauns. The National Leprechaun Museum of Ireland is a privately owned house of the exhibit dedicated to these mini-Irish people of old.

Chapter One - HISTORY

Exhibits include an optical illusion tunnel, a Giant's Causeway of Northern Ireland wooden replica, and a room with unusually oversized furniture to give the experience of a leprechaun's view of the world.

It's more of an immersive storytelling activity than a museum. Talented tour guides will entertain you with tales of Irish folklore and mythology. Learn about the Tuatha de Dannan, leprechauns, and, of course, Irish fairies. And at the end, there's a gift shop, of course.

The Irish Times has comically dubbed it the "Louvre of leprechauns."

Chapter One - HISTORY

PART 6 - WEATHER

WEATHER = COMPLAINING = GENETICS

Being Irish means complaining about the weather is passed onto you at birth. During the winter season, with the sun starting to go down by 4 PM, the inevitable daily gasps over how dark it's gotten will start to be heard. Complaining about how dark it is, how cold it is, how gloomy and wet it is, is the true Irish winter experience.

RAIN

It rains A LOT!

Rainfall is common around the island, but particularly near the west coast, where precipitation falls greater than once every two days on average. Rainfall is common throughout the entire island, although it is especially frequent and heavy near the slopes of the western highlands, where annual rainfall reaches 2,000 millimeters (80 inches).

Rainfall in Galway, on the west coast, averages 1,150 mm (45.5 in) a year. On the southern coast, in Cork, it averages 1,200 mm (48 in).

The eastern part of the country where Dublin is located experiences the least rainfall: annual rainfall is roughly 760 mm (30 in).

Chapter One - HISTORY

WINTER

From December to February, the weather is cool but not frigid. The sky is frequently gloomy, rain is common, and the most extreme low-pressure systems can result in wind storms.

Temperatures are just above freezing at night, but range from 7/8 °C (45/46 °F) in the inland to 8/10 °C (46/50 °F) anywhere along coastlines during the day.

During winter's milder periods, when southerly air currents reach Ireland, temperatures can exceed 15 °C (59 °F) even in January.

There are no large mountain ranges in Ireland; however, rain can change to snow above 400/500 meters (1,300/1,600 feet) in the Wicklow Mountains to the south of Dublin, and more infrequently in the western highlands- a thousand meters (3,300 feet) in height.

Cold waves are uncommon, but in some circumstances, minor frosts can be experienced on clear evenings. For roughly twenty days per year in Dublin and up to 50 days in inland areas, nighttime temperatures drop past freezing (0 °C or 32 °F), usually by a few degrees.

However, there are times when a cold snap is more severe than usual. For example, near Christmas time 2010, the temperature dipped to -15 °C (5 °F) in the interior north-central portions of Ireland and dropped to -11.5 °C (11 °F) on the western outskirts of Dublin.

Chapter One - HISTORY

WINTER IN EACH PROVINCE

Each province and region within has unique weather temperature and patterns, but on average, the country receives 12-13 days of snowfall and just 4-5 days of snow cover.

Broken down by each of the 4 provinces

ULSTER province to the north, near Northern Ireland, averages 20 days w snowfall a year, but only 3-4 days of snow cover.

MUNSTER province in the south averages 5-10 days of snowfall annually and just 1 day of snow cover.

LEINSTER, the eastern province across the Celtic/Irish Sea from Wales, experiences between 10-15 days of snowfall each year but just 3-4 days of snow cover.

CONNACHT (or Connaught) to the west averages 18 days of snowfall with just 3 days of snow cover.

SPRING

March through May, is initially frigid and continues to be quite cool or cold in April and occasionally in May; the temperature normally begins to warm up only in the second half of May, while nights can still be pretty cold. On the other hand, Spring is the (relatively) driest and sunniest season of the year.

Chapter One - HISTORY

Temperatures, consider an average between the 3 cities of Dublin in the East, Slingo in the North and Shannon in the west -

Mid-March = Lows of 4C or 38F to Highs of 10C or 51F

Mid-April = Lows of 5C or 41F to Highs of 12C or 54f

Mid May = Low of 8C or 46F to Highs of 14C or 57F

SUMMER

Summer temperatures are moderate June to August, with average highs in the north of 17/18 °C (63/64 °F) and 19/20 °C (66/68 °F) in the remainder of Ireland. Rainfall is also common during this time of year.

When the Azores High (atmospheric pressure), from the Portuguese Azores located 1400km west of Lisbon, passes over Ireland, there may be brief intervals of bright weather and mild temperatures. These temperatures can reach or surpass 25 °C (77 °F) in these conditions; however, it almost never hits 30 °C (86 °F).

On June 26, 1887, at Kilkenny Castle, Ireland's warmest ever temperature of 33.3 °C (91.9 °F), was recorded. While in the range of possibility, such an old data set is not very dependable.

Chapter One - HISTORY

Summer is the best time to visit Ireland because it is the warmest of the year. Rainfall is common, and the air is often very cool (especially in June), so you are advised to bring a jacket and umbrella (or rather a raincoat because it often rains with the wind). On the bright side, the days are long, and you will see glimpses of the sun through the rich clouds.

For example, while in Dublin, one can expect winter daylight to average just 2 hours per day, then spring shows 5, summer as much as 6, before dimming, with Autumn averaging 3.5 hours.

The temperatures are still pleasant in September, but the sky is frequently gloomy, and the days quickly become shorter than in previous months.

AUTUMN

Ireland's autumn is overcast and rainy, with little sunshine. Winds can also be fairly severe during this time of year, particularly in the later months.

Pack suitable rain gear as well as lots of warm layers. Although an umbrella is required, you may find it more practical to bring along a hooded garment.

Chapter One - HISTORY

Late fall is one of the wettest seasons of the year. Average rainfall over much of the island in September is 60m or 2.4 inches, October & November is 100mm or 4 inches. Average daytime highs by November fall to 10 °C (50 °F), 50F with lows of 5 °C (40 °F).

The weather is still pleasant in September, and the days are relatively long. September is a fantastic time for photography because of the contrast between the lingering purple heather, summer greens, and a touch of late-season colors.

Although October might be rainy, it is the time of changing leaves and wildlife activity. The month of November is dry but cooler than the past two. November is the greatest autumn month for witnessing the Northern Lights because of better skies and longer nights.

Chapter One - HISTORY

PART 7 - RANDOM FAST FACTS #1

GEORGE BERNARD SHAW

George Bernard Shaw, an Irish writer, had a revolving office where he could face the sun in the winter and have more shade in the summer.

SEAN'S BAR

Ireland is home to the world's oldest bar! From Guinness Book of Records, Sean's Bar is Ireland's "Oldest Pub," with a history reaching back to 900AD.

GAELIC PLACES

Thousands of present-day locations, building names in Ireland can be traced back to Gaelic, Celtic, and English names.

LONGEST NAME

Galway's Sruffaunoughterluggatoora is the longest name for a river in Ireland.

LONG TOWN NAME

Muckanaghederdauhaulia is the longest title of a town in Ireland.

ST. PATRICK'S REAL NAME

St. Patrick's given name was not 'Patrick.' It was Maewyn Succat.

NEWGRANGE WINTER SOLSTICE

Light passes through the burial tomb for around 19 minutes a day during the winter solstice.

GUINNESS POUR

A perfect Guinness pint takes 119.5 seconds to pour.

Chapter One - HISTORY

NATIONAL SYMBOL
The Republic of Ireland is the only nation in the world whose national symbol is a musical instrument.

HARPS
Trinity College in Dublin houses some of the world's oldest harps.

3 SYMBOLS OF IRELAND
The Celtic Cross, Green Shamrock, the Harp (musical instrument) are the three most recognized Celtic symbols of Ireland.

GERMAN SHAMROCKS
In the early 1980s, Germany attempted to include the shamrock into its national identity, just like Ireland.

SNAKE FREE
Even before Saint Patrick, there were no snakes in Ireland. Because Ireland is an island nation, many creatures found on mainland Europe are unable to access the Emerald Isle. Therefore, most animals, creatures, and creepy crawlies are limited in variety

chapter two
ST. PATRICK'S DAY, & PARADES

PART 1 - LEGEND OF ST. PATRICK

ST. PATRICK WAS WELSH?

Ireland's patron saint is St. Patrick, who many people assume was himself an Irishman, but the real McCoy was actually British. He was born in roughly 390 AD to an aristocratic Christian family somewhere in Roman Britain, most likely in Wales of all places.

MAEWYN SUCCAT

Most historians believe Saint Patrick was born "Maewyn Succat" but changed his name to "Patricius" after becoming a priest.

Maewyn Succat is about as Welch as it gets.

DETAILS ABOUT THE TALE OF ST. PATRICK

At the age of sixteen, Patrick was captured by raiders in northern Britain and transported across the Irish Sea by pirates, where he was sold into slavery. Following a mystical vision and escape from six years of servitude, Patrick returned to Ireland armed only with a mystic's faith to convert the island to Christianity, eliminating slavery and human sacrifice in the process.

Chapter Two - ST. PATRICK'S DAY, & PARADES

Patrick returned to Ireland against his family's wishes in 433 A.D. His mission in Ireland would endure the final 30 years of his life, baptizing Irish pagans, ordaining priests, and erecting churches and monasteries.

Patrick, in particular, decried and denounced the enslavement of Irish women while also praising their valor and fortitude.

ST PATRICK AND SHAMROCKS

In popular Irish folklore, Saint Patrick used the shamrock to represent the Holy Trinity during his Missions across Ireland. The attachment of St. Patrick to the shamrock is heavily debated among all leagues of scholars.

ST. PATRICK'S SNAKES

As legends have it, Saint Patrick is well-known for driving snakes out of Ireland, defeating tough Druids in magical competitions, and using the shamrock to explain the Christian Trinity to the pagan Irish. It's a fantastic tale, but unfortunately none of it is factual.

The shamrock mythology, like the miracle fights against the Druids, arose decades after Patrick's death. And the snakes; the Emerald Isle never had any in the first place. Fossil record shows as the Emerald Isle have never been home to snakes since it was too cold for reptiles during the Ice Age. Since then, snakes have been kept at bay by the surrounding seas, with none having attempted the trip from neighboring lands.

FEAST DAY

Sources say the celebration of St. Patrick dates back to the 10th century. At the time, the holiday was known as "Feast Day of St. Patrick". The celebration's name came from taking place during the Catholic time of Lent, but on this special day, the Irish were excused from their dietary restrictions so they may feast. Cabbage and ham was the preferred menu.

PART 2 - LEPRACHAUNS

TYPICAL LEPRACHAUNS ARE DISNEY

Although Leprechauns and St. Patrick's Day go hand in hand, it was only when Disney introduced the mythical little beings in the 1959 film "Darby O'Gill and the Little People" that those in America made the connection. Different from the Leprechauns of the ancient tales, the happy, luck-of-the-Irish leprechaun we see today is a Hollywood invention.

LEPRACHAUNS

The legendary Leprechauns are considered Fairies. These are not happy leprechauns; they are considered unfriendly and untrustworthy. They live in the forests, make shoes and have lots and lots of gold.

PART 3 - ST. PATRICKS DAY CELEBRATIONS

ST. PATRICK'S DAY IN DUBLIN

Every year the Capital of the Emerald Isle attracts 1 million to its parade and festivities, 500,000 being visiting tourists. The city really comes alive and, for Americans, would resemble a New Orleans Mardi Gras-style atmosphere. As well, many buildings in the city will be lit in emerald green.

PARADE

Starting at noon, the parade along O'Connell Street will feature artists and marching bands from around the world.

MANY PINTS

Dublin's pubs have been known to serve more than 15 million pints of Guinness during the multi-day celebration.

GOV'T BUILDING ARE CLOSED

Becoming a national holiday in 1903, all financial institutions, post offices, and government facilities will be closed.

FLORIDA WAS 1ST TO HONOR ST. PATRICK WITH A PARADE

St. Augustine, Florida, claims to be the birthplace of the St. Patrick's Day parade celebration as far back as 1601.

Chapter Two - ST. PATRICK'S DAY, & PARADES

Historian J. Michael Francis, History Professor at the University of South Florida, learned from citizen records of a parade held March 17th, 1601 honoring the Irish saint.

In 1600 the St. Augustine area was a Spanish colony under the Irish vicar Ricardo Artur. Documents read of cannon fire in honor of San Augustin but also mentioned the 2nd saint in Saint Patrick.

A year later, in 1601, St. Augustine held a parade in honor of St. Patrick.

BOSTON'S FIRST ST. PATRICK'S PARADE

On March 17, 1737, members of the newly founded Charitable Irish Society marched along Tremont Street from King's Chapel to the Old Granary Burying Ground to celebrate Ireland's patron saint, St. Patrick. However, it wasn't until the flood of Irish immigrants into Boston in the 1850s that large-scale Irish parades began.

Boston's locals may know the parade began in Boston Common and made its way about the downtown, crossing the Charlestown-Cambridge bridge, returning to Boston, and then crossing the South Boston Bridge.

SOUTH BOSTON'S TURN AT THE ST. PATRICK'S DAY PARADE

The St. Patrick's Day procession was transferred from downtown Boston to South Boston in March 1901, where it was merged with another significant event, Withdrawal Day, which commemorates the British troops' evacuation of Boston in March 1776.

Linking St. Patrick and a day for honoring the military makes sense for the South-side Bostonians.

South Boston has a long history of sending its sons and girls to fight in the military, dating back to the Spanish-American War and the American Civil War and continuing in the modern day.

CHICAGO RIVER RUNS GREEN

The Chicago St. Patrick's Day celebration is known worldwide as the day the Chicago River is dyed green. This event began more than 60 years ago when then-Mayor Richard J. Daley and the Plumbers Union moved the procession from the city's South Side to the downtown, taking place on the Saturday before St. Patrick's Day.

Chapter Two - ST. PATRICK'S DAY, & PARADES

THE BIG APPLE HOSTS THE BIGGEST PARADE

New York City's St. Patrick's Day Parade is the country's largest. The inaugural parade, which took place on March 17, 1762, was comprised of Irish men serving in the British Army. In perspective, this 1762 parade happened a full 14 years prior to America's 1776 Day of Independence.

Since its beginning, and for many years to follow, the parade would pass by the Old St. Patrick's Cathedral (now known as the Basilica), which is located at the corner of Mott and Prince Streets in the SoHo neighborhood.

Today, the parade marches up Fifth Avenue and is greeted by His Eminence, Cardinal Timothy Dolan, Archbishop of New York, as he stands on the steps of the cathedral.

THE GREAT PARADE OF PITTSBURGH?

Since 1869, the city of Pittsburgh PA has celebrated St. Patrick's Day with a parade, which has grown to become one of the largest in the world. The celebration involves over 23,000 participants, including marching bands, politicians, and a slew of Irish-heritage organizations. The event is enjoyed by more than 200,000 spectators, all of whom are "Irish for the Day."

2ND OLDEST USA PARADE CITY?

Second, only to the New York City St. Patrick's Day parade is, believe it or not, the Savannah Georgia celebration (continually) since 1824.

The city was founded in 1733 on the banks of the Savannah River and grew to become the colonial (Provincial) capital of Georgia and, later, the first state capital of Georgia.

While 1824 may be the first public parade on record, prior to that year, two private processions had been documented in Savannah. The first was in 1813 when members of the Hibernian Society (founded in 1812) marched to the Independent Presbyterian Church. The second was a private procession organized in 1818 by the Fencibles, a local military unit.

NEW ORLEANS ST. PADDY'S PARADE....MARDI GRAS STYLE

In New Orleans, St. Patrick's Day is a week-and-a-half-long extravaganza that begins on the 17th of March. There will be three parades and two renowned block parties with all kinds of fun since just one of them won't suffice in New Orleans.

Chapter Two - ST. PATRICK'S DAY, & PARADES

The Irish Channel, a community known for the high population of Irish families in the area, is one of the hottest spots to be on St. Patrick's Day. The day-long street party is located near the Garden District just outside Downtown New Orleans and the French Quarter.

On the Sunday before St. Patrick's Day, the annual Parade marches down Magazine St. and St. Charles Ave.

The parade's marchers and riders will have lots of green beads and doubloons to wear and toss, as well as throwing the ingredients for Irish stew. As a result, onions, potatoes, cabbage heads, and carrots take flight, then taken home and cooked by spectators.

At the end of the night's celebration, everyone dunks a shamrock into their last glass of whiskey and toasts the saint. This is known as "Drowning the Shamrock," a good luck charm that is supposed to bring you good fortune for the coming year.

PART 4 - ST. PATRICKS DAY FOOD, BEER, FACTS

PADDY'S NOT PATTY'S
St. Paddy's Day is the (proper) informal abbreviation of St. Patrick's Day. St. Patty's is incorrect as Patty is the abbreviation for the female name Patricia. The Irish take pronunciation of its special day very seriously.

NORTH AMERICAN BEER SALES
No surprise, March 17th is a big day for beer sales. It's said that North American beer sales spike an average of a whopping 174% on St Patrick's day.

HAM, NOT CORNED BEEF, FOR ST. PATRICK'S DAY FEAST
The traditional Ireland St. Patrick's Day festival feast of corned beef and cabbage contains no corn. The name refers to the huge grains of salt that were once used to cure meats and were referred to as "corns."

The Irish would traditionally enjoy ham and cabbage, but when immigrating to NA, they found the locals enjoying corned beef as the protein of choice on their green day.

Corned beef and cabbage, very synonymous with the Irish, they say, though it's actually an American invention.

TOWNS IN AMERICA NAMED AFTER SHAMROCKS AND IRISH:

Mount Gay-Shamrock, WV

Shamrock, OK

Shamrock, TX

Shamrock Lakes, IN

Emerald Isle, NC

Irishtown, IL

Clover, SC

Clover, IL

Clover, MN

Clover, PA

Cloverleaf, MN

PART 5 - FAST FACTS – ST. PATRICK (DAY)

FATHER FIGURE
St. Patrick = Patricius, which means "Father Figure."

PATRICK'S OCCUPATION
Patrick worked as a sheepherder in Ireland for six years before escaping.

4-LEAF ODDS
You have a 1 in 10,000 chance of discovering a four-leaf clover.

$ SPENT ON ST. PATRICK'S DAY
$4.6 Billion was spent celebrating St. Patrick's Day in America, 2012.

MARIAH'S BETTER HALF
Singer Mariah Carey is part Irish.

BEER CONSUMPTION

2x the money and 2x the beer is consumed when St. Patrick's Day lands on a Saturday.

WEEKENDS ARE BEST
3 in 10 Americans attend a St. Patrick's Day celebration or bar when the day falls on a Friday, Saturday, or Sunday.

Chapter Two - ST. PATRICK'S DAY, & PARADES

TRAFFIC DEATHS

103 Traffic fatalities occurred on St. Patrick's Day in 2009. 47 involved motorists with blood alcohol above the legal limit of 0.08. In perspective, 122 people died from drunk drivers on New Year's Eve-day, 2009.

AMERICAN ST. PATRICK'S DAY MEAL

A traditional meal on St. Patrick's Day in America consists of corned beef and cabbage. Ireland serves ham.

RELIGIOUS DAY

St. Patrick's Day began as a religious holiday.

MONTH OF MARCH FOR THE IRISH

1995 March was declared as the official Irish-American heritage month in America.

YEAR OF BIRTH

St. Patrick was born in Wales around 386 AD

TIME OF DEATH

St. Patrick died March 17th, 461 AD and was buried in Downpatrick, Co. Down, Ireland (now, Northern Ireland), located 34 km or 21 miles south of Belfast.

Chapter Two - ST. PATRICK'S DAY, & PARADES

NICKNAME
St. Patrick's nickname was "Paddy."

LARGEST PARADE IN AMERICA
The Largest St. Patrick's Day Parade in America is in New York City. As many as 150,000 marchers and 2 million spectators take in the festivities.

BOSTON & DUBLIN PARADE'S
Boston's St. Patrick's Day parade attracts 600,000-1M viewers while Dublin hosts 750,000, in contrast.

% OF BOSTON IRISH
From various surveys, as few as 21% to as many as 40% of people in Boston claim to be of Irish heritage.

BOSTON PARADE DETAILS

Boston's St. Patrick's Day parade starts at 1 PM, lasts 2.5 hours, and stretches 3.5 miles.

chapter three

EMMIGRATION/IMMIGRATION, BOSTON, AMERICA, ARGENTINA

Chapter Three - EMMIGRATION/IMMIGRATION, BOSTON, AMERICA, ARGENTINA

PART 1 - IRISH EVERYWHERE

IRISH AROUND THE WORLD

The eighty million Irish living abroad is one of the largest in the world. There is a substantial Irish diaspora in over 70 countries, and as many as 36 million people have claimed Irish ancestry on US census forms alone.

Ireland has a long history of mass emigration, and a notable current emigration wave beginning in 2008. Some have returned to their homeland, while others have not.

MORE IRISH OUTSIDE IRELAND THAN INSIDE

It is estimated that there are more than 13x the number of folks with Irish ancestry residing outside of Ireland than there are in Ireland. 80 million of Irish ancestry live abroad, but only 5 million live in Ireland and nearly 2 million in Northern Ireland.

IRISH IN AMERICA

Census Bureau data shows that most often 32-33 million Americans, or 9-10%+ percent of the country's total, identify as Irish.

Chapter Three - EMMIGRATION/IMMIGRATION, BOSTON, AMERICA, ARGENTINA

PART 2 - EMIGRATION TO AMERICA

FIRST TO AMERICA

The Irish first settled in the United States in the 1700s. These people were predominantly Scots-Irish and, for the most part, settled into a farm-based way of life in Virginia, Pennsylvania, and the Carolinas. This is considered the first wave of Irish emigration.

GREAT POTATO FAMINE

The next, 2nd, and much larger, more consistent wave occurred during the late 1800s, initiated by the Great Potato Famine.

This catastrophic famine, still remembered in Ireland and around the world today, led to countless Irish seeking a better life. This was the nation's single biggest exit of people ever witnessed. Cobh, a port in Co. Cork, at one time called Queenstown, saw 2.5 million citizens pass through the ports and board ships for trans-Atlantic voyages.

SETTLING IN AMERICA

Ireland's men and women leaving their home weren't always the poorest of the Irish as they had the means to travel to new lands, but upon arrival in America, these weary travelers were for the most-

part penniless and considered poor and unable to choose their end destinations. Because of this, a huge number of Irish stayed in the ports they originally arrived in, mainly New York City or Boston. These large numbers of destitute Irish created the unofficial Irish ghettos.

UNSKILLED LABOR

A large number of those who arrived were unskilled, but fortunately, America needed a lot of manual labor, so these over-flowing Irish ghettos provided thousands of workers, cheap labor. These people of circumstance helped build America's infrastructure of roads, railways, and cities.

HOW MANY IRISH CAME TO AMERICA?

The 1890 census shows Irish numbered over 190,000 in New York City, 260,000 in Boston, and as many as 124,000 in Illinois, mainly in and around Chicago.

HOW MANY AMERICANS OF IRISH ANCENSTRY?

Recent public census reports have shown that 33.3 million Americans (10.5% of the population) have Irish ancestors, connections, or heritage, and certain areas retain a huge connection to the Emerald Isle. Two recent and noticeable examples include 24% of people living in Boston considering themselves of Irish descent and 45% of those in Breezy Point, a neighborhood of Queens, New York.

Chapter Three - EMMIGRATION/IMMIGRATION, BOSTON, AMERICA, ARGENTINA

LARGEST US CITY METRO AREAS WITH IRISH ANCESTRY

Boston, Massachusetts 22.8%

Pittsburgh, Pennsylvania 16.2%

Philadelphia, Pennsylvania 14.2%

Louisville, Kentucky 13.2%

Portland, Oregon 11.9%

Seattle, Washington 11.65%

Buffalo, New York 11.23%

Nashville, Tennessee 9.8%

Kansas City, Missouri 9.66%

Raleigh, North Carolina 9.5%

Cleveland, Ohio 9.43%

Saint Paul, Minnesota - 9.4%

Baltimore, Maryland 9.14%

Cincinnati, Ohio 9.05%

Austin, Texas 8.5%

Charlotte, North Carolina 8.4%

Chicago, Illinois 8%

Memphis, Tennessee 7%

New Orleans, Louisiana 6.8%

Chapter Three - EMMIGRATION/IMMIGRATION, BOSTON, AMERICA, ARGENTINA

PART 3 - PORTS OF EMIGRATION

COBH

Nearly six million men, women, and children left Ireland between 1848 and 1950 in of a better life elsewhere.

This amazing number of people is made even more fascinating when you learn that 2.5 million of them, or near half of all emigrants, left through Cobh, County Cork.

The view of St Colman's Cathedral, standing large over the harbor, was certainly a lasting recollection of Ireland for many who never returned.

DERRY

Due to a dearth of records for the entire country prior to 1820, The majority of these emigrants came from County Derry and adjoining County Antrim, and they were going for Philadelphia, Pennsylvania, or Saint John, New Brunswick, or Quebec, Canada.

Chapter Three - EMMIGRATION/IMMIGRATION, BOSTON, AMERICA, ARGENTINA

LIVERPOOL

Liverpool has traditionally been a port city influenced by a steady stream of Irish given the proximity, only a short ride across the Irish Sea.

Despite the fact that this was always the case, both during and after the Great Famine of the 1840s, numbers unavoidably increased. Since then, and far into the early twentieth century, Liverpool has served as a vital stopover for so many Irish families on their way to other territories.

OTHER PORTS

Throughout the numerous waves of emigration from Ireland, many other ports, such as Belfast and Galway, were utilized.

Despite the fact that Irish emigration dates back to the 1700s, the focus tends to be on more recent flows due to a lack of records.

Chapter Three - EMMIGRATION/IMMIGRATION, BOSTON, AMERICA, ARGENTINA

PART 4 - BOSTON IMMIGRANTS

Over the last 150+ years, the children of Irish immigrants have absorbed Irish culture, history, and way of life so that it's now hard to imagine Boston without a Celtic twist.

BOSTON 1654

The first Irish, primarily of Presbyterian origin, landed in Boston in 1654 and were largely put into near slavery work. Those who showed, but avoided indentured work, lived in areas surrounding Boston, including settlements such as Belfast, Maine, - Derry, New Hampshire, - and Londonderry Vermont (all replicated names of Ireland cities).

1ST ST. PATRICK'S DAY

These first 100+ years, many of the Irish had to fend for themselves, resulting in the start of the Charitable Irish Society on March 17th, 1737. Of note, this is the first documented occurrence of Saint Patrick's Day in Boston.

THE GREAT HUNGER 1845 - 1849

Thousands of Irish, looking for a new home and hope of a better future, set sail across

Chapter Three - EMMIGRATION/IMMIGRATION, BOSTON, AMERICA, ARGENTINA

the Atlantic in the infamous "Coffin Ships" and came ashore with nothing but their clothing. The vast majority of arrivals were unskilled and thus used for low-paid, manual labor and unwanted jobs throughout the city.

NOT WELCOME
The large influx of Irish was met with anger, disdain, and often resulted in violence as "Paddys," "Micks," & "Bridgets" became targets and labelled "Non-American". This tension grew into a movement known as the "Know-Nothings," with many preaching against Boston's new immigrants during the 1840s and 1850s.

CIVIL WAR & POLITICS
Because of the large number of Irish participating in the Civil War, fighting for the Union, in addition to 2nd and 3rd generations entering municipal politics, the Irish were ultimately accepted and integrated into the modern, more liberal version of Boston we all know today.

TODAY'S BOSTON
Boston's Irish population is the city's biggest single ethnic community. With some estimating 23% of its population of Irish descent, Boston retains its status as a center of Irish-American culture and history.

With reference to percentage alone, Boston is the most Irish city in America, excelling beyond other cities the likes of Chicago and New York!

Chapter Three - EMMIGRATION/IMMIGRATION, BOSTON, AMERICA, ARGENTINA

IRISH TRANSFORMED BOSTON TO CATHOLIC

The influx of European immigrants to the Boston metro area, formerly a Puritan bastion, transformed the city forever in the 19th century. Following the Great Irish Famine, the initial wave of immigration was overwhelmingly Irish. When they arrived, they turned Boston from a Protestant, Anglo-Saxon city into a Catholic one.

BOSTON'S "MISSING FRIENDS"

From 1831 through 1920, the Boston Pilot Newspaper had a "Missing Friends" column in which readers advertised their search for "lost" Irish friends and family members in the US. These ads are now searchable online on Ancestry.com, thanks to the efforts of Boston College researchers. Interesting facts like where they were born, when they left, what they did for a living, and other personal information may be found in the adverts.

Chapter Three - EMMIGRATION/IMMIGRATION, BOSTON, AMERICA, ARGENTINA

PART 5 - AMERICAN CIVIL WAR

200,000 IRISH FOUGHT

In the American Civil War, it's thought that nearly 200,000 Irish Americans took up arms, with 150,000 for the Union and 40,000 for the Southern Confederacy.

VOLUNTEERS

Many enlisted voluntarily, considering America as their new home, but others were compelled to do so by the divisive Enrollment Act of March 3, 1863.

The Union's provocative moves resulted in brutal clashes, such as the Detroit Race Row on March 6, 1863, as well as the New York Draft Riots on July 13-16, also in 1863.

FOUGHT FOR FREEDOM

Despite the concerns that dominated the Civil War on a political level, the Irish simply sought to preserve their liberties and better financial prospects for their families and following generations.

Chapter Three - EMMIGRATION/IMMIGRATION, BOSTON, AMERICA, ARGENTINA

FIGHTING FOR THE SOUTH

Surprisingly, in the years when the Irish were considered dirt poor and shunned by many of America's established and elite, some on the Confederate side thought the southern states were more open and friendly to them.

IRISH REGIMENTS

Many Irish citizens organized their own regiments and battalions. The Union side featured the 69th NY State Volunteers, the 90th Illinois Infantry Regiment, and Irish Bridge, while the Confederacy side had the 24th Georgia Volunteer Infantry and Louisiana Tigers.

Despite the divisions, the Irish fought valiantly for both sides and suffered great losses during the conflict.

IRISH AT GETTYSBURG

While no official data exist, it is believed that a significant number of Irish soldiers died among the 165,000 troops involved during the legendary Battle of Gettysburg on July 1-3, 1863.

Chapter Three - EMMIGRATION/IMMIGRATION, BOSTON, AMERICA, ARGENTINA

GREAT SEAL OF THE U.S.

County Derry's Charles Thompson, who served as Secretary of the Continental Congress and lived to 94, was part of the design committee for the Great Seal of The United States.

STAR-SPANGLED BANNER

Irish-Americans credit Irishman Turlough O'Carolan for composing the original Star-Spangled banner.

O'Carolan was a well-known traveling blind Irish harpist from Co. Meath.

DECLARATION OF INDEPENDENCE

Three of the eight foreign individuals involved in signing the Declaration of Independence were from Ireland. On July 4th, 1776, James Smith, George Taylor, and Matthew Thornton etched their names into history.

Chapter Three - EMMIGRATION/IMMIGRATION, BOSTON, AMERICA, ARGENTINA

PART 6 - ARGENTINA

500,000

While the number of Irish living abroad is often underestimated, recent statistics suggest that there are at least 500,000 Irishman and women living in Argentina. That number represents about 15% of the country's total population. However, the number of Irish immigrants may be even higher.

19TH CENTURY MIGRATION

The majority of these people migrated from Ireland to the United Kingdom in the 19th century, and many of them claimed to be British because Ireland was part of the United Kingdom when they arrived. In addition to claiming Irish ancestry, these people have integrated into Argentine society through mixed bloodlines.

Chapter Three - EMMIGRATION/IMMIGRATION, BOSTON, AMERICA, ARGENTINA

PART 7 - RANDOM FAST FACTS #2

SHAMROCK TRADEMARK
The Irish government has trademarked the shamrock for use as a nation symbol.

EDUCATION
Ireland has one of the world's most educated workforces.

SHAMROCK USAGE
Ireland's national symbol, the shamrock, is used on a variety of ways: Aer Lingus, Irish postal stamps, and the call sign "SHAMROCK" for air traffic control.

"POGUE MAHONE"
"Pogue Mahone" was the early name of the well-known band Pogues.

This translates to the Irish Gaelic phrase "póg mo thóin," which literally means "kiss my arse."

DAILY GUINNESS PINTS
Every day, the St James' Gate Brewery in Dublin produces about 3,000,000 pints of Guinness.

CLIFFS OF MOHER IN MOVIES
The Cliffs of Moher have appeared in films such as Harry Potter and the Half-Blood Prince, Mackintosh Man, and the Princess Bride.

Chapter Three - EMMIGRATION/IMMIGRATION, BOSTON, AMERICA, ARGENTINA

YOUNG DEMOGRAPHIC

More than 50% of the population of Ireland is under the age of 30.

GREAT FAMINE

A major crop of Ireland's, the potato, failed in the 1840s, resulting in the Great Famine.

FAMINE = DEATH AND EMIGRATION

Between 1846 and 1851, 1M of Ireland's people perished of famine and disease, while some say 2M people emigrated.

LESS WILD ANIMALS

Because Ireland is so remote from the rest of Europe, it lacks some common European animals like moles, weasels, polecats, and roe deer.

HIGH # OF LEVEL 3 EDUCATION

53.5% of 30-35-year-olds in Ireland have completed a 3rd level education (Uni-College) vs. 40% European avg.

Chapter Three - EMMIGRATION/IMMIGRATION, BOSTON, AMERICA, ARGENTINA

SUBMARINE
John Philip Holland invented the submarine in Ireland.

DRACULA AUTHOR
Abraham "Bram" Stoker was an Irish author, being best known for his 1897 Gothic horror book Dracula.

chapter four
NOTRE DAME

Chapter Four - NOTRE DAME

PART 1 - ORIGINS, PEOPLE

CATHOLIC PRIESTS

A group of French-speaking priests founded Notre Dame in 1842. It was historically a Catholic institution, having established America's first Catholic law school in 1869 as well as the nation's first Catholic engineering school in 1873. In 1887, the football program began.

IRISH ENROLLMENT

Because of the school's Catholic background, several Irish immigrants wanted to enroll their children in order to advance economically and socially. Thus began the origin - correlation that leads one down the road towards the meaning of the nickname "Fighting Irish."

FOUNDER

Few people are aware that Notre Dame's founder, Father Sorin, intended to establish the institution in the warmer climate of California. However, he was snowed in at the current home of Notre Dame while heading westward.

Chapter Four - NOTRE DAME

He decided to put his travel plans on hold until the weather cleared, which never did.

ND PRESIDENT AND U.S. PRESIDENT

From 1946 to 1952, John J. Cavanaugh served as President of Notre Dame. He was a personal acquaintance of the Kennedys and served as their unofficial chaplain. Father John was also a personal friend of the first Catholic President of the United States, JFK. Over the years, he presided at several family weddings, aided Kennedy's presidential campaign, and attended Kennedy's funeral until his 1979 passing.

PART 2 - "FIGHTING IRISH"

"FIGHTING IRISH" ORIGIN

Despite the fact that "The Fighting Irish" is one of the most well-known names in American and international sports, the origins and beginnings of the team are still a source of contention.

Many people believe the name comes from an Irish immigrant soldiers' brigade that fought for the Union during the Civil War. This group of brothers became known as "The Fighting Irish," and their ties to Notre Dame were deep. So deep in fact that the brigade's chaplain, Father William Corby, subsequently became the college's 3rd President!

"FIGHTING IRISH" IS ANTI-CATHOLIC

Some believe the name originated as a snide remark made against the university's athletic teams. Northwestern University students screamed "Kill the Fighting Irish" during a football game in 1899. Anti-Catholicism and anti-immigrant attitudes were widely expressed in the United States at the time, and Notre Dame was a perfect target for ethnic slurs because it was predominantly populated by ethnic Catholics — mostly Irish, but also Germans, Italians, and Polish.

Chapter Four - NOTRE DAME

"FIGHTING IRISH" 1909

The name is also said to have come about as a result of the school rebounding from a half-time drubbing against Michigan in a 1909 game and being christened "The Fighting Irish" by an attending journalist.

"FIGHTING IRISH" IRELAND'S 1ST PRESIDENT

Another explanation connects the name to Eamon de Valera, Ireland's first president.

During his fleeing from Ireland after the Easter Rising of 1916, de Valera traveled to the United States in 1919, specifically to Notre Dame (school) on October 15, 1919, where he was greeted with much fanfare. Many people believe that this visit was the catalyst for the nickname.

NOTRE DAME – EARLY NAMES

Notre Dame and its sports teams were known by several names during a transitional time in history between the late 1800s and early 1900s. They have given the nicknames "Rovers" and "Ramblers" because of their propensity to travel across the USA to play the greatest teams in the country.

The team was also called the "Terriers" at one stage, in honor of the Irish Terrier dog breed.

OFFICIALLY "FIGHTING IRISH"

The nickname "The Fighting Irish" gained popularity through time, but it wasn't until 1927 that the school formally acknowledged and supported

Chapter Four - NOTRE DAME

it. Reverend Matthew Walsh, Notre Dame's 11th President, accepted the name on behalf of the squad.

The link between the sports teams and college has grown in popularity as American Football has increased in popularity.

The Emerald Isle Classic, a collegiate exhibition game staged in Dublin starting in 1996 is the best example of this.

Chapter Four - NOTRE DAME

PART 3 - CAMPUS

LOCATION
Officially located in Notre Dame, Indiana. This is a census-designated area just to the north of South Bend, a city in St. Joseph County. Saint Mary's College & Holly Cross College share the grounds.

GOLDEN DOME
The Golden Dome atop the Main Building is encrusted with 23.9-karat gold leaf. During a re-gilding, students frequently notice flakes of gold on the surrounding grass.

GROTTO
The Grotto of Our Lady of Lourdes is a 1/7 sized miniature replica of the famous French shrine in which the Virgin Mary manifested to Saint Bernadette 18 times in 1858.

HARRY POTTER INSPIRATION
The South Dining Hall's architecture looks like a medieval Guild Hall from Harry Potter, prompting annual Harry Potter-themed dinners since 2009.

Chapter Four - NOTRE DAME

DORMS

The school uses a "stay dorm" system. Approx. 80% of the students live on campus. Because there are no co-ed dorms, your dorm essentially becomes your frat by default.

Dorm room selection is based on class and GPA. Seniors, Juniors, and Sophomores are prioritized. Freshmen make do with the leftovers.

DORMS & VIETNAM
The first dorm was built on campus at the time of the Vietnam war. At the time, it was dubbed Sorin Hall and used for classes as students boycotted University events.

TOUCHDOWN JESUS
ND's main library building, "Theodore Hesburgh Library," opened in September 1963 and displays a multi-story mural of Jesus, now commonly known as "Touchdown Jesus."

Chapter Four - NOTRE DAME

FOOTBALL STADIUM

Notre Dame Stadium, home of The Fighting Irish (American) football team, was built in 1930, costing $750,000 ($19.8M in 2022), seats 77,500, has natural grass, and is dubbed "The House that Rockne Built" after famed coach Knute Rockne.

NHL CLASSIC

Notre Dame's outdoor football stadium hosted the 2019 NHL Winter Classic - A January 1st, regular season professional hockey played outdoors between the Boston Bruins and the Chicago Blackhawks. Boston won 4-2.

PART 4 - NOTRE DAME TRADITIONS

MARSHMALLOWS

The senior class brings in hundreds of thousands of marshmallows during the final home game of the year. They throw them at each another in the student section during games. The tradition began as a joke, but now it's become an annual event. Many tales speculate its beginnings but this tradition's true origins remain a mystery.

STAIRS

Students are not permitted to climb up the primary staircase of the Main Building on campus before they have graduated, as is customary. They have access to different stairwells. Graduation is traditionally marked by numerous photographs taken from the stairwell as students ascend the stairs for the very first time.

SHREK

Sections of the Notre Dame campus have been suggested as the inspiration for the film Shrek. Some say Notre Dame graduates who worked on the script included honors to their alma mater. Lord "Farquaad," for example, sounds like the "Far Quad," a location on the Notre Dame campus. The kingdom of "Dulac" is said to be called after

Chapter Four - NOTRE DAME

the student handbook at the school, "du Lac." The Hesburgh Library on campus looks a lot like the castle in the movie.

NOT ALWAYS A LEPRECHAUN

The present mascot at Notre Dame is a leprechaun; however, this hasn't always been the case. Before the leprechaun, the school was represented by Irish terrier dogs. The concept of a cheering leprechaun was first presented in 1960 and became the official mascot in 1965. Currently, pupils must audition for the position of mascot by donning a green suit and traditional Irish country hat.

CHAMPIONS DROUGHT

Since the football "polling" era starting in 1936, only one school has more

championships than Notre Dame's eight — Alabama. The Crimson Tide have 14, and as recently as 2020. Notre Dame has won 11 recognized national championships as far back as 1943 and as recently as 1988. They've technically won 22 and list 10 as co-national wins. 7 Heisman winners have played for the team. The Fighting Irish are currently in their longest (national) title drought ever. Despite this, Notre Dame games continue to be broadcast by NBC, first airing in 1991.

LOVE ON CAMPUS

On the Notre Dame campus, there are two significant marriage superstitions. One, it is said that kissing under the Lyons Arch will lead to marriage. The second is a hand-held figure-eight stroll around both St. Mary's and St. Joseph's lakes.

BOOKSTORE BASKETBALL

The Notre Dame Bookstore Basketball Event is the world's largest outdoor 5-on-5 tournament. In this student-run tournament, over 500 teams and 4900 students play in both an open and a women's division. Some groups take it very seriously, whereas others dress up and have fun. The two-month event takes place rain or shine in March and April.

INTRAMURALS

Intramural sports are very popular. Each dorm has its own colors and cheers. Most sports, including swimming, have campus-wide championships.

The school offers both 11 v 11 full padding and full contact intramural football and 6 v 6 full padding and full contact intramural hockey.

GOLDEN HELMETS

The "golden dome" helmets are an essential part of Notre Dame's football uniform. According to legend, the paint for the helmets contains actual gold flakes from the gold dome atop the main building on campus. The team have worn these gold helmets since the 1950s

Chapter Four - NOTRE DAME

RUDY WAS OFFSIDE

"Rudy," a sports film released in 1993, has become a classic. It tells the narrative of Daniel "Rudy" Ruettiger, a Notre Dame football player who surmounted many challenges. Rudy ultimately gets to play in the final scenes of the film and scores a sack. Didn't he? Many people have looked into this play and believe Rudy was aligned in the neutral zone, which renders him offside. In real life, the play would have been flagged, and the sack would have been nullified.

PART 5 - FAST FACTS -NOTRE DAME

PROPER NAME
The full name of the University of Notre Dame = University of Notre Dame du Lac

1842
Established November 26th, 1842

MOTTO
Motto - Vita Dulcedo Spes (Latin) meaning Life, Sweetness, Hope

PRIVATE
Officially classified as a "Private research university."

SIZE
Campus size = 1,261 acres or 5.1 sq km

HALLS
The school has 33 residence halls.

ENDOWMENT
The endowment is $20.3 billion, one of the largest of any school in the U.S. Operating budget is $1.5 billion.

ACCEPTANCE
The school's acceptance rate is just 19% (2022)

STUDENTS
12,700 students: 8,700 undergrads and 4,000 post grads. 1,400 staff

Chapter Four - NOTRE DAME

TUITION
Typical tuition fees to the school cost a student $59,000 (2021)

FRATS
Fraternities and sororities are not permitted on campus (only a few academic honor clubs and the Knights of Columbus)

RECTORS
Usually, two each dorm and at least one of them being a priest or a nun.

MOVIES
The football-related films "Knute Rockne, All American" and "Rudy" were both filmed at Notre Dame.

MARRIAGE SUPERSTITION #1
Legend has it if a male and female student join hands and walk the campus in figure 8 around the two lakes, they will marry.

MARRIAGE SUPERSTITION #2
According to legend, if two people of the opposite sex kiss under the campus' Lyons' arch, they will marry.

HEISMAN
Notre Dame football athletes have won the Heisman trophy for top collegiate player 7x, being the most from any one school.

NFL HALL OF FAMERS
13 Pro Hall of Fame football players attended Notre Dame.

chapter five
NORTHERN IRELAND

Chapter Five - NORTHERN IRELAND

PART 1 - WHAT IS NORTHERN IRELAND

WHAT IS IT?

Northern Ireland is considered and named a country, or province, or region depending on who is referencing it, that is part of the United Kingdom, according to various definitions.

There is no official or legally defined term to describe what Northern Ireland is. Generally, a writer's description of the region as provincial, a region, county, or other reflects their political affiliation. The UK gov't generally documents the land as a "Province," but the European Union says "Region."

UK'S CONNECTION

The United Kingdom governs NI, yet Northern Ireland makes its own set of laws. The Republic of Ireland or "Ireland", on the other hand, is a sovereign state.

Northern Ireland, the Republic of Ireland, and the United Kingdom signed a peace deal in 1998. The

Chapter Five - NORTHERN IRELAND

Irish Constitution was revised to remove the Republic's territorial claim to Northern Ireland.

DIFFERENCES OF OPINION

Major newspapers and government sites like universities identify with

the name "Ulster" (a province) as in "University of Ulster" while many other media outlets use "North of Ireland" or "The North" (very popular) as well as "Six Counties." (Ulster has 9 counties, 6 in NI, 3 in Ireland)

QUEEN RECOGNITION

Northern Ireland is part of the British Empire and therefore recognizes the sitting Monarch (Elizabeth II), and their Anthem is "God Save the Queen."

LOCALS SAY IT LIKE THIS

Northern Ireland, as said by the locals, can be "Norn Iron," informally and affectionately, and most when referring to their sports teams.

Chapter Five - NORTHERN IRELAND

PART 2 - ORIGINS, OLD NORTHERN IRELAND

NORTHERN IRELAND VS. ULSTER

Northern Ireland is on occasion referred to as Ulster, despite the fact that it consists of only 6 of the 9 counties that comprised the medieval-time named Irish province.

1600S - ANGLO-SAXONS AND NORMANS

Thousands of Scottish Presbyterians were forcibly resettled in Ulster during the 17th century, during the period known as the "Ulster plantation." English military garrisons were founded, resulting in the institutionalization of ethnic, spiritual, and ideological differences that later culminated into violent conflicts.

1920 ACT

The Government of Ireland Act 1920 established Northern Ireland as a separate legal entity on May 3, 1921. The majority of Northern Ireland's inhabitants were unionists who wished to remain within the United Kingdom of Great Britain.

Meanwhile, the majority of Irish nationalists and Catholics in Southern Ireland, as well as a sizable minority in Northern Ireland, sought a unified, independent Ireland, resulting in the Republic of Ireland or simply "Ireland."

More than 500 were killed, and 10,000 became refugees in the violence of 1920-22, leading to Northern Ireland's - Republic of Ireland's separation.

ST. ANNE'S CATHEDRAL

Located on Donegall Street, Belfast, is St Anne's Cathedral, popularly known as Belfast Cathedral. Belfast's Cathedral Quarter revolves around it.

Chapter Five - NORTHERN IRELAND

PART 3 - "THE TROUBLES"

The Republic of Ireland and Northern Ireland were torn apart by conflict from the years 1968 to 1998. This period is known as "The Troubles."

NICRA

"Many people believe that only nationalists and unionists fought in "The Troubles" war. When actually individuals and organizations positioned themselves in the middle, such as NICRA - Northern Ireland Civil Rights Association.

BOMBINGS

During The Troubles," almost 10,000 bomb assaults happened in Ireland and the United Kingdom.

BELFAST

The Belfast area was home to a large number of civilian deaths (approximately 1,500) during the Troubles bombings. Belfast, the capital and most populous city of Northern Ireland, is located on the east coast of the country, on the banks of the River Lagan. The capital was one of

Chapter Five - NORTHERN IRELAND

the most hazardous cities in the world during the violence that accompanied Ireland's partition, and notably during The Troubles: in the 1970s and 1980s, it was one of the most dangerous cities in the world.

BULLETS
Armed forces shot roughly 30,000 plastic bullets during 1981's Hunger Strike. The following eight years, only 16,000 plastic bullets were fired.

INJURIES
During "The Troubles," an estimated 107,000 persons suffered physical injuries.

U2 SONG
Bloody Sunday was written by U2 in response to "The Troubles."

MUSICIANS INSPIRED
Many performers, including Phil Collins, Sinead O'Connor, U2, Morrissey, and Flogging Molly, drew inspiration from Northern Ireland's Troubles.

CONCLUSION TO VIOLENCE
The Good Friday Agreement, signed on April 10, 1998, is widely regarded as the conclusion of "The Troubles."

PART 4 - TODAY'S NORTHERN IRELAND

WHERE IS IT?

Northern Ireland, which is located in the northeastern part of the island of Ireland, shares a border with the Republic of Ireland on the south and west sides of the island.

Northern Ireland is barely 13 miles from the coast of Scotland at its closest point.

POPULATION & SIZE

The population is estimated to be at 1.9 million people as of April 2021.

Northern Ireland, separate from Ireland, consists of 30% of the total of the Island of Ireland's population. It is also 3% of the UK's 67 million population.

The country's overall area is 14,130 km2 (5,460 square miles). It takes up around one-sixth of Ireland's land area.

DEMOGRAPHICS

The country is 98.2% Caucasian. The next highest ethnic group is Asian at 1.1%

YOUNG POPULATION

Northern Ireland has a young population, with close to half of its people below the age of 30.

Chapter Five - NORTHERN IRELAND

MONEY
As part of the British Empire, Northern Ireland uses the Pound Sterling (£)

CITIES
Major cities include Belfast (pop: 344K), Londonderry (Derry) (pop: 84K), Lisburn (pop: 45K), Newtonabbey (pop: 66K), Craigavon (pop: 16K)

AFFORDABLE
A house in Northern Ireland costs on average £141,463 ($190,092 USD).

CAPITAL
The capital city is Belfast. With a population of 344,000, it is Northern Ireland's largest city and 12th largest among United Kingdom cities.

OFFICIAL LANGUAGE
English is the official language and people speak it as a first language.

Irish and Ulster Scots are considered regional languages. The Gaelic language is taught in some schools and some regions in both Ireland and Northern Ireland. Individuals are encouraged to learn and use it to maintain traditions.

CHRISTIAN MAJORITY
The majority, 82.3%, are recognized as Christian, while 10.1% claim no religion.

Chapter Five - NORTHERN IRELAND

NATIONAL DAY
National Day, like July 4th for the USA and July 1st for Canada, Northern Ireland's day is March 17th, St. Patrick's Day.

POLITICS
The current leader is First Minister Paul Jonathan Given of the DUP - Democratic Unionist Party.

ECONOMICS
The GVA or Gross Value Added of all goods and services produced/supplied is £49 billion or $66 billion USD. £26,000 or $35,000 per capita.

OLYMPIC IDENTITY
Northern Ireland athletes may choose to compete at the Olympics for either Ireland or Great Britain.

UNEMPLOYMENT
NI experienced unemployment as high as 17.2% in 1986 before modernizing its economy with tech, investment banks, and deals with Ireland and the UK.

PART 5 - FAMOUS LANDMARKS AND LOCATIONS

MOUNTAINS, LANDSCAPES

Northern Ireland was frozen over during the last ice age and many times before, as evidenced by the enormous coverage of drumlins in Fermanagh, Armagh, Antrim, and Down.

Stunning landscapes may be found across the province, ranging from the craggy coastlines of the northeast to the mild weather fruit-growing districts of Armagh.

As a result of its geographical location, Northern Ireland has had a lengthy history of arrivals and emigration, notably Celts from Europe and Vikings, over the centuries.

LOUGH NEAGH

Lough Neagh, with an area of 391 square kilometers (151 square miles), is the geographic centerpiece of Northern Ireland's landscape. It is the largest freshwater lake on the island of Ireland and the largest freshwater lake in the British Isles.

FAMOUS GIANT'S CAUSEWAY

The Giant's Causeway is a 40,000-square-foot area of interlocking basalt columns formed by an old volcanic fissure eruption. It's in County Antrim, on Northern Ireland's north coast, about 4.8 kilometers (3 miles) northeast of Bushmills. The Causeway dates back more than 50 million years. In 1986, UNESCO made it a World Heritage Site.

DUNLUCE FORTRESS

Dunluce Fortress, the seat of Clan McDonnell, is a now-ruined medieval castle in Northern Ireland. The castle is bordered on all sides by extraordinarily steep drops, which may have played a role in attracting early Christians and Vikings to the site where an early Irish fort formerly stood.

BELFAST CASTLE

Belfast Castle is located 120 meters (400 feet) above sea level on the hills of Cavehill Country Park in Belfast. Its location allows for unobstructed views of Belfast City and Belfast Lough.

LED ZEPPLIN

The Ulster (concert) Hall in Belfast's city center hosted the first live performance of Led Zeppelin's renowned song "Stairway To Heaven."

CARRICK-A-REDE ROPE BRIDGE

The Carrick-a-Rede Rope Bridge connects the mainland to Carrickarede, a small island off the coast of Ireland. It stretches for 20 meters (66 feet) and rises to a height of 30 meters (98 feet). The National Trust owns and cares for the bridge, which is primarily used as a tourist attraction.

GAME OF THRONES – DARK HEDGES

Bregagh Road in County Antrim, Northern Ireland, has an avenue of beech trees known as "The Dark Hedges." The trees create an ambient tunnel that has become a major tourist attraction since being seen in the HBO series Game of Thrones.

TOLLYMORE FOREST PARK

Tollymore Forest Park, NI's first national park, is located at the foot of the Mourne Mountains and spans 630 hectares (1,600 acres), with scenic views of the mountains and the coastline at Newcastle.

HAUNTED CASTLE

Ballygally Castle, now serving as a hotel, is Northern Ireland's most haunted location.

CRANES

The famous Samson and Goliath cranes in Belfast are the world's largest free-standing cranes, standing 106m or 348ft.

KILLYLEAGH CASTLE

Killyleagh Castle in County Down is Ireland's oldest continuously inhabited castle.

LACK OF TREES

NI is the least forested region of the UK and Ireland and even Europe. The terrain was extensively forested with native trees such as yew, oak, ash, elm, aspen, hazel, willow, alder, birch, and Scots pine until the end of the Middle Ages. Only 8%

of Northern Ireland is now covered in woodland, the majority of which is non-native fir plantation.

PART 6 - FAST FACTS – NORTHERN IRELAND

FLAG
There is just one legally recognized flag in Northern Ireland: The Union Jack.

DRIVING
Just like Britain, Northern Irelanders drive on the left.

MAC
Many Irish names start with "Mac." A direct translation of this word is "son of."

SURNAME – "O"
Last names frequently begin with the letter "O," which in Gaelic signifies "grandson of."

SETTLERS
Settlers from Scotland and England began coming to Ireland in the 17th century.

OBEL
The Obel Tower, at 85m or 279 ft, in Belfast (City), is Ireland's tallest structure.

MOUNTAIN HIGH
Slieve Donard, 850m, is Northern Ireland's highest peak (2,790 feet).

Chapter Five - NORTHERN IRELAND

OLD TAVERN

Ireland's oldest thatched tavern, the Crosskeys Inn in County Antrim, dates back to the 16th century.

RMS TITANIC

The Titanic, the ill-fated ship, was built in Belfast, 1908-12.

PUBLIC DRUNKENESS

Being intoxicated in public is considered illegal in Northern Ireland.

FREE BEER

At one time, peasants were permitted to drink ale for free, according to the Tippling Act of 1735. Regrettably, this legislation has now been abolished.

RIVER BANN

The longest river in Northern Ireland is the River Bann, and is 129 kilometers long (80 miles).

BRONZE AGE FOR BELFAST

Belfast City is located on ground that has been inhabited since the Bronze Age.

NARROW BAR

The Glass Jar, located in Belfast, is the city's narrowest bar.

WOMAN – QUEEN'S UNIVERSITY

Women could occupy any post at Queen's University in Belfast 12 years before they could study at Oxford's Universities, Oxford (UK)

Chapter Five - NORTHERN IRELAND

AMERICAN PRESIDENTS
Many American presidents, including Jackson (7th), Buchanan (15th), and Arthur (21st), have Ulster - Province / Northern Ireland ancestors.

FAMOUS NORTHERN IRELANDER'S
Writer C.S. Lewis (Belfast), Actor/Filmmaker Kenneth Branagh (Belfast), Poet Seamus Heaney (Castledawson), and actor Liam Neeson (Ballymena) are just a few of the renowned persons that were born in Northern Ireland.

PEACE WALL
Belfast's famous Peace Walls separate Catholic and Protestant neighborhoods from one another.

DUNLOP TIRES
John Dunlop of Belfast devised the pneumatic tyre (tire), which had a major impact on the development of automobiles, lorries, bicycles, and airplanes.

RECORD BRACELET

A Northern Ireland schoolboy was granted a Guinness World Record in February 2020 after creating a 6,292-foot-long loom band bracelet.

RAIN

Northern Ireland has 157 rainy days per year on average, which is fewer than Scotland, but it's more than Dublin!

SUNDAY IS NOT MOVIE TIME

Going to the movies on Sundays is technically illegal in Northern Ireland. This is due to a law passed in 1991 regarding the observance of the Sabbath.

EGG INSPECTIONS

By law, an "Officer of the Ministry officially approved by the Ministry either generally or on a particular occasion" can inspect eggs in transit.

chapter six
PUBS, ALCOHOL, GUINNESS

Chapter Six – PUBS, ALCOHOL, GUINNESS

PART 1 - ALCOHOL CONSUMPTION

The stereotype is the Irish drink a lot, particularly beer and whiskey. Although they love their beer, Guinness, and hot whiskey on a cold day, the Irish are far from the heaviest of drinkers, a characteristic in which they are often associated.

6TH IN THE WORLD

At 93 (some say 131) liters per person, on average, Ireland citizens rank 6th in the world for beer consumption. The Czech Republic is #1 at 188.6 liters per person on average, over 2x what Ireland drinks. Indonesia's citizens consume the least, with just 0.7 liters per capita per year.

446 LITERS = #26

Ireland overall consumes 446 million liters of beer per year. This is the 26th most of any country in the world. China is #1, consuming 43.27 billion liters a year. Consider that China has 1.4B people, which is 200x times Ireland's/Northern Ireland's less than 7M people.

MULLED WINE AND HOT WHISKEY

A sign to the locals that its winter in Ireland - Mulled wine (AKA spiced wine) or hot whiskey is the drink of choice whether you're a visitor in a host's home or a patron in a pub. The Irish describe it as a boozy beverage made with red wine or whiskey, mulled spices, and often raisins and served hot or warm.

PART 2 - TOP 10 BEST IRISH BEERS

(Credit: meanwhileinireland.com)

TOP 10 BEST IRISH BEERS

10 - KILKENNY IRISH CREAM ALE

A traditional smooth ale with a variety of flavors, including toffee, caramel, and toasted nuts.

9 - O'HARA'S IRISH STOUT

Basic and brilliant, it is believed to taste exactly as Irish stouts have traditionally tasted, staying faithful to the Irish brewing tradition.

8 - WICKLOW WOLF ELEVATION PALE ALE

A delicious ale craft beer using grapefruit and pineapple flavors that lend to it being a well-loved Irish craft beer.

7 - RASCALS HAPPY DAYS SESSION PALE ALE

It contains a tropical flavor with undertones of passion fruit, mango, melon, and orange, making it a delight to sip.

6 - HARP LAGER

A highly recognizable worldwide brand(ing), this is a fantastic brew for anyone who likes a quality conventional lager.

5 - GALWAY BAY ALTHEA APA

Another tropical beer with elements of papaya, peach, and mango, this wonderful Irish craft beer is similar to Rascals Happy Days Session Pale Ale.

Chapter Six – PUBS, ALCOHOL, GUINNESS

4 - BEAMISH IRISH STOUT

Beamish, which predates even Guinness, was the very first Irish stout. Dark chocolate & coffee flavors combine to make a delicious brew.

3 - MURPHY'S IRISH STOUT

Murphy's is lighter than traditional Stout's like Guinness and Beamish, while tempting drinkers iced mocha taste buds.

2 - SMITHWICK'S RED ALE

Count Smithwicks among Ireland's oldest beers. Having been made by Franciscan monks in the 14th century, its hoppy flavors delight. The red ale is the fan-favorite.

1 - GUINNESS IRISH STOUT

Make no doubt about it, this deliciously creamy brew is Ireland's most famous drink.

PART 3 - IRISH PUBS "DO'S & DO NOT'S"

When in Rome do as the Romans. And when in Ireland, join the Irish at their local pub, but be mindful of their pub's casual, friendly and traditional nature when ordering and enjoying a Guinness.

SEATING

Don't be pretentious, find yourself a seat. The majority of bars and pubs have a "seat yourself" rule of order.

DRINK MENUS

Drink menus are few and far between. If you don't know what you want go to the bar, look at the fridges, shelves and draft handles and spirit pumps.

ORDER AT THE BAR

With few exceptions, patrons order at the bar. Don't wait for a waitress.

THE BARTENDER SEES YOU

Avoid shouting, waving hands, whistling. Bartenders are professionals and scope the crowd for who arrived at the bar and when. Flagrant gestures signal "tourist" and service may be sparce the rest of the night

Chapter Six – PUBS, ALCOHOL, GUINNESS

TIPPING

Tipping is rare and is not required, although welcomed if given for great service. Bar staff are compensated well so do not have to rely on gratuity. "Tipping" is far more common in North American and "no tipping" is standard for European services.

ROUNDS

Buying rounds of drinks for your party or others within the pub are common place. A good habit is to give as well as receive.

Friends and even that night acquaintances engage in round-buying. Each member of a party takes turns to buy the group drinks, often of the same

brand-kind. This also helps lessen those crowding the bar with orders.

SLOW POURS

Guinness is famous for a perfect pour at 45 degrees taking 2min. So, each patron counting on a pint of this authentic Irish brew requires patience.

Chapter Six – PUBS, ALCOHOL, GUINNESS

PART 4 - GUINNESS

1 IN 4 BEERS

While we're all aware of the stout's huge profile in the country and prominence in pubs, there's also plenty of other tempting lagers and ales available. In the Emerald Isle, however, at least one of every four beers (1/4 of all beers) ordered is a Guinness. How deliciously predictable.

10,000,000

Every day, 10 million pints of Guinness are brewed in Dublin.

ARTHUR GUINNESS, 1759

Guinness beer's story began in 1759 when Arthur Guinness acquired a 9000-year lease on what is now the St James Gate Brewery.

St James Gate became Ireland's biggest and most successful brewery dating all the way back to the 1830s. The brewery quickly evolved into a city within a city, even constructing its own railway to transport barrels.

1ST YEAR FOR GUINNESS

In its first production year, Guinness brewing only shipped 6 1/2 barrels of beer from Ireland across the water to England.

Chapter Six – PUBS, ALCOHOL, GUINNESS

MANY GUINNESS RECIPES
When one thinks of Guinness, they think of the original and world-famous Irish Stout. Other popular recipes of Guinness include multiple Porter's, a smooth, and even a non-alcoholic option.

Guinness now is not the same as the original brewing company and its beers. Guinness recipes have developed throughout time, and new types of Guinness have emerged to suit various preferences.

STOUT
One of the most popular types of Guinness stout is Guinness Foreign Extra Stout accounting for 45% of the brand's total sales.

HARP
Guinness branding displays a harp prominently above its lettering. The harp is the national symbol of Ireland.

5-GENERATION = OPERATIONS
For five generations, operations (not ownership) of the Guinness company have been passed down from father to son and are still running strong.

DIAGEO OWNERSHIP
Today, Guinness is owned by London England Headquartered multinational brewing conglomerate Diageo. At one time was the world's largest distiller before China's Kweichow Moutai overtook it in 2017.

PART 5 - GUINNESS MUSEUM

DUBLIN'S GUINNESS BEER ATTRACTION/MUSEUM

Since its opening in the year 2000, the Guinness Storehouse has been Irelands most popular tourist attraction, having hosted 20 million visitors.

The Storehouse is a seven-story building with a glass atrium designed in the shape of a pint of Guinness.

1ST FLOOR

The 1st floor exhibits the 4-ingredient beer recipe and the brewery's founder Arthur Guinness. Other floors showcase the history of the product, advertising, drinking awareness programs, and messaging.

TOP FLOOR BAR

The top, 7th floor contains the Gravity Bar where guests can enjoy a complimentary pint of Guinness while enjoying views of Dublin.

PART OF ORIGINAL BREWERY

The Storehouse is in the original fermentation plant (for yeast) of Guinness's St. James Brewery, in full use from the 1830s until 1988 when a new plant was

constructed near the River Liffey. The original early 19th-century building was the first multi-storied steel frame building constructed in Ireland.

Recent additions to the building and exhibits were designed by renowned museum design specialists Event-Communications of London.

QUEEN'S VISIT

A state visit to Ireland in May 2011 included a visit to the Storehouse by Queen Elizabeth II and Prince Philip.

Chapter Six – PUBS, ALCOHOL, GUINNESS

PART 6 - GUINNESS & NIGERIA

NIGERIANS CONSUME MORE GUINNESS THAN IRELAND

40% of the world's Guinness consumption happens in Africa. Nigeria, specifically, is the home of 3 Guinness breweries of its own and is the largest consumer in Africa and 2nd country or region overall consumer behind only the UK.

NIGERIAN CONNECTION

Guinness, brewed in Nigeria since 1962.

NIGERIAN MARKET

Guinness has been sold in Nigeria since 1827, primarily in glass bottles, and became an enormous market for the brewer.

NIGERIAN BREWERY

Guinness Nigeria, a unit of the United Kingdom's Diageo PlC, was founded in 1962 with the construction of a brewery in Ikeja, Lagos. This brewer was the company's first outside of Ireland and the United Kingdom to produce Guinness. This pioneering facility had a capacity of 75 million bottles or 150,000 barrels of beer per year.

Other breweries, such as the Benin City brewery in 1973 and the Ogba brewery in 1963, have since opened and operated under the Guinness label.

PART 7 - FAST FACTS - GUINNESS

PINTS PER DAY
5.5 million pints of Guinness are consumed each and every day around the world

PINTS CONSUMPTION
13 million pints of Guinness are consumed by those around the world celebrating on St. Patrick's Day.

SOLD AND BREWED
Guinness is sold in over 100 countries and brewed in almost 50 countries.

IRISH STOUT
Guinness Irish stout was being consumed in Africa as early as 1827, with possible bootlegging happening years before.

JAMAICA
Jamaica is one of the most avid drinkers and consumers of Guinness.

NUTRITION
Draft Guinness Pint (16oz - 473ml) contains 210 calories and 18.2 grams of carbohydrates.

An Extra Stout Guinness (12oz - 355ml) contains 155 calories and 17 grams of carbohydrates.

Chapter Six – PUBS, ALCOHOL, GUINNESS

SCIENTISTS

Guinness was the first brewery of its kind to employ scientists to hone tastes and processes.

NUTRITION – GUINESS VS OTHER BEVYS

Guinness is thought to be high in calories.

Drinks with similar / more calories (155) than 12oz or 355ml of draft Guinness:

Anchor Porter = 205 cal

Orange Juice = 183 cal

Sam Admas Bostom Lager = 160 cal

Coors Original beer = 148 cal

Dos Equis = 145 cal

Budweiser = 143 cal

Skim Milk = 135 cal

chapter seven
DRACULA, MUSIC, FAMOUS PEOPLE

Chapter Seven - DRACULA, MUSIC, FAMOUS PEOPLE

PART 1 - DRACULA

AUTHOR

In 1897 Bram Stoker, a Dubliner, wrote the Gothic horror novel, a fictional account of the famous vampire Count Dracula. Sir Henry Irving, a friend of Stoker's, was the real-life basis for the vampire's persona.

DRACULA = CHIEFTAIN ABHARTACH

Count Dracula was the result of 20 years of Victorian literature's vampire legends. Dracula is claimed to have been influenced by the earlier Irish legend of Abhartach, a wicked chieftain who resurrected from his tomb every night to drain the blood of his victims after being deceived by his subjects and murdered by the hero Cathrain.

STOKER WAS A THEATRE MANAGER

Many don't realize Stoker, the famous novelist was primarily the personal assistant to classic English Literature theatre actor Sir Henry Irving better known as J.H. Irving. Irving was the owner and primary actor of the Lyceum Theatre on Wellington Street in the City of Westminster in central London. Part of Stoker's assistance to Irving was as Business Manager of the Lyceum Theater.

Chapter Seven - DRACULA, MUSIC, FAMOUS PEOPLE

PART 2 - MUSIC

The Slane Festival is an annual concert held 45km northwest of Dublin.

8TH MARQUESS CONYNGHAM

At the initiative of the 8th Marquess Conyngham, the Slane Festival (or Slane Concert) has been hosted (nearly) yearly on the grounds of Slane Castle since 1981. The castle is/was owned and festival sponsored by the Earl of Mount Charles (Courtesy title - 1974-2009). The concert usually occurs in August though it has happened some years in May. Marquess Conyngham, the castle owner, wanted the event to have "real, not manufactured bands"; thus, many mainstream pop acts are not invited.

MUSIC ACTS

Among the musicians who have headlined Slane are:

Bryan Adams

Bob Dylan

Foo Fighters

Madonna

U2

Queen

The Rolling Stones

Robbie Williams

Metallica

Chapter Seven - DRACULA, MUSIC, FAMOUS PEOPLE

PART 3 - THE POGUES

IRELAND'S 2ND MOST POPULAR BAND

Billions in the world have heard about and listened to the famous Irish band U2. Bono and crew are world-renowned musicians, but have you ever heard of arguably Ireland's #2 greatest band?

POGUES

The Pogues, the famous Irish band's original name was "Pogue Mahone," which translates to "kiss my arse" in Irish Gaelic.

Pogue Mahone was a Celtic punk band created by Shane MacGowan and headed by him throughout their early years of prominence. In 1991, MacGowan departed the band because of drinking difficulties. The band stayed together from 1982 until 1996, broke up, and then reformed again from 2001 to 2014.

Their most famous works include "Fairy Tale of New York," which reached #2 on the UK charts in 1988, and 1986's piano ballad "A Rainy Night in Soho."

POGUES MUSIC IN HBO'S THE WIRE

'Body of an American' was first published as part of the 1986 EP 'Poguetry in Motion'. This icon song intros with a tin whistle and accordion before transitioning into MacGowan's account of the tumultuous death of Irish-American boxer Big Jim Dwyer, who had been carried back to Ireland to be buried. On HBO's 'The Wire,' boozed-up officers of the Baltimore Police Department would play the song, belting out the chorus, "I'm a free-born man of the United States of America."

Chapter Seven - DRACULA, MUSIC, FAMOUS PEOPLE

PART 4 - IRISH DANCING

Irish dancing, like storytelling, Gaelic games, and traditional music, is an important element of Ireland's culture, history, and heritage.

Whether you reside on the Emerald Isle, are a member of the Irish diaspora, or simply admire Irish culture from afar, odds are you've seen Irish dancing in some form.

STYLE FROM LACK OF SPACE

Irish dance is characterized by a lack of upper-body movement and rapid, frenzied footwork. The limited venues available for public dancing during its early years contributed significantly to the growth of this style. Local barns, bars, and whatever else was available served as dance events.

ROUTINES AND COMPETITIONS

Dependent on the dancers and parties participating, the dancing can be solo or group, and it can be done for social, competitive, or performance goals.

Step routines, set dancing, social ceili routines, and dances known as jigs, reels, and step dances are all part of Irish dancing.

Chapter Seven - DRACULA, MUSIC, FAMOUS PEOPLE

ORIGINS

Dancing is thought to have arrived in Ireland from the Druids and Celts. Druids were reported to do circular routines around sacred trees, and Celts celebrated the "Aonach" (Great Festival) with group dances at the famous Hill of Tara.

The origins of what we now know as Irish dancing may be traced back to the 17th century when it was inspired by English Country routines and Classic French Quadrille dances.

DANCE INSTRUCTORS

Traveling "dance instructors" began to appear in Ireland in the 17th century, instructing locals technique and flair as they went from town to village. The growth of Irish traditional music coincided with this period, and the two cultural forms today go hand in hand.

WORLD CHAMPIONSHIPS

The foundation of the Gaelic League in 1893, the Irish Dancing Committee in 1930, and the Irish Dancing World Championships in 1970 marked the beginning of modern Irish dancing.

The World Championships are still held every year; more than 6000 dancers from 30+ countries compete each year.

Chapter Seven - DRACULA, MUSIC, FAMOUS PEOPLE

RIVERDANCE

However, for many people, modern Irish dancing means only one thing: Riverdance.

The iconic Irish dancing show debuted at Eurovision in 1994, starring champion performers Jean Butler & Michael Flatley, having a 15-year run of worldwide popularity.

DANCING TODAY

Hundreds of Irish dancing organizations and contests may still be found all over Ireland on a grassroots basis.

Chapter Seven - DRACULA, MUSIC, FAMOUS PEOPLE

PART 5 - 6 CELEBRITIES NOBODY KNOWS HAVE IRISH ANCESTRY

TOM CRUISE

Tom Cruise is a leading star with memorable roles in films such as "Top Gun" "Jerry Maguire" as well as "Born on the Fourth of July," and has always spoken proudly of his Irish heritage.

Cruise traced his roots back to Dublin, and when visiting recently, he received an honorary Certificate of Irishness from the Irish gov't.

MERYL STREEP

On her maternal side, Streep's great-great-grandparents are from County Donegal, located in the northwest corner of the island.

In honor of her Irish heritage, she christened her daughter Grace Strain after her great-great-grandmother.

People of Ireland will recall her work in the film 'Dance at Lughnasa,' in which she demonstrated her exceptional acting abilities by delivering a convincing Donegal accent as well as her Irish dancing abilities.

Chapter Seven - DRACULA, MUSIC, FAMOUS PEOPLE

MARIAH CAREY

International superstar performer Mariah Carey's connection is through her mom, Patricia Hickey.

"My mother's so Irish. She loves Ireland, waves the flag, and sings When Irish Eyes Are Smiling. And that's great."

WILL FERRELL

Funnyman Will Ferrell has Irish ancestors from the agricultural rich northern located in County Longford. Will's family emigrated and modified their surname from Farrell to Ferrell.

The comedian has been known to boast about his Irish roots, one time saying he's so committed to being Irish that he'll continue to drive on the left side of the road no matter how dangerous or illegal.

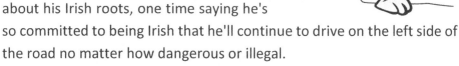

ROBERT DENIRO

Actor Robert De Niro, best known for his roles in Taxi Driver and The Godfather films, is universally considered one of the finest actors of all

time. Edward O'Reilly, De Niro's great-great-grandfather, was an Irish immigrant to the United States. When De Niro was just 19, he traveled to Ireland with no money slept in barns, fields, and even homes of a few kind strangers. A trip to trace his roots that he says he'll never forget.

CHRISTINA AGUILERA

Mega singing sensation Christina Aguilera experienced her childhood in Irish American neighborhoods in New York and Pennsylvania.

Although she has a Latin surname and constant fuss to explore this Latin side in music, she just as much values her Irish ancestors on her mother Shelly Kearns's side.

PART 6 - RANDOM FAST FACTS # 3

TITANIC PASSENGER LIST

The Belfast List shows that 2,225 individuals boarded the Titanic.; 1,317 passengers, and 908 crew members. Only 713 people survived.

EURO ADOPTION

In 2002, Ireland was among the first 12 E.U. Countries to adopt the euro currency.

CLIFFS OF MOHER

The Cliffs of Moher in Ireland are more than 320 million years old.

HALLOWEEN ORIGINS

Halloween came from the old Celtic harvest celebration of Samhain on Oct 31st, which marked the end of summer, and All Saint's Day on Nov 1st blending to form Halloween.

WHITE HOUSE DESIGN FROM AN IRISHMAN

An Irishman named James Hoban designed and built the American White House after winning an architecture competition in 1792.

Chapter Seven - DRACULA, MUSIC, FAMOUS PEOPLE

TITANIC CONSTRUCTION

The Titanic was built 3 years by 3,000 workers. Its huge hull was kept

together by 3 million rivets. In today's money, a first-class ticket would have been €89,000 ($99,000 USD).

TOP DRINKERS OF GUINNESS

Surprisingly, despite being the birthplace of Guinness, Ireland does not sell the most of this stout in the world! Britain is #1, Nigeria is #2, and Ireland is #3.

KILKENNY WITHCRAFT

In the late 13th century, Dame Alice Kyteler of Kilkenny was the first person in Ireland to be found guilty of witchcraft. She was suspected of poisoning to death all four of her husbands. Today, you can eat at Kyteler's Inn in Kilkenny, which is still run by her family.

Chapter Seven - DRACULA, MUSIC, FAMOUS PEOPLE

MORE IRISH IN USA

33+ million people in the United States are of Irish heritage, which is 7 times the population of Ireland.

1ST PARADE IN NYC

The first St. Patrick's Day held in New York City happened in 1762 when a group of Irish troops who were homesick for their homeland marched through the city.

NYC IRISH POPULATION

According to a 2008 American Community Survey, New York City has 414,943 persons of Irish descent.

PATRICK'S OF STATEN ISLAND (NY)

Patrick is the name of 1 in every 161 residents of Staten Island, New York.

chapter eight

TV & MOVIES

Chapter Eight - TV& MOVIES

PART 1 - INDUSTRY, TAX BREAKS

From Star Wars to Vikings, many films and television shows have been made in Ireland. Although not Irish in story, they display the Emerald Isle in all its glory.

TAX BREAKS = JOBS

As a result of Screen Ireland's marketing efforts and significant tax incentives, the Irish film industry has seen modest growth in recent years. According to the Irish Film Board, this industry has grown from employing 1,000 individuals six or seven years ago to employing well over 6,000 people today. Today the industry's worth approximately €557.3 million to the country's GDP. Because Ireland is mainly anglophone, most films are filmed in English, though others are created entirely or partially in Irish.

WORLD-CLASS DIRECTORS

In 2000, Ireland could only boast but a few well-known moviemakers' directors. By 2010, Ireland had more than a dozen filmmakers and authors with substantial and growing worldwide acclaim. Ireland is now amassing filmmaking talent to equal the level of impact it has traditionally had in literature and culture.

PART 2 - BRAVEHEART

FILMED IN IRELAND NOT SCOTLAND

It is without a doubt many film watchers favorite Hollywood film and just happens to be filmed in Ireland.

With breathtaking grandeur, this epic tale chronicles the events of the legendary thirteenth-century Scottish hero William Wallace, portrayed by award-winning actor and director Mel Gibson.

After suffering a personal tragedy at the hands of English soldiers, Wallace organized the Scottish people against England's King Edward I.

LOCATIONS

Filming took place in Scotland and on the eastern coast of Ireland in the counties of Kildare, Meath, and Wicklow.

A great majority of the fight sequences in Braveheart were filmed in Ireland, which surprised many visitors to Scotland after the film's release. Just like the battle scenes, Bective Abbey in County Meath was used to film all shots resembling London. The Curragh Plains in County Kildare were used to film the Battle of Stirling Bridge, and Trim Castle in County Meath was used to film the sequences set in York.

PART 3 - SAVING PRIVATE RYAN

SPIELBERG'S EPIC WAR FILM

The epic 1998 American war film written by Robert Rodat and directed by Steven Spielberg had filmed in Ireland.

The movie is famous for its vivid depictions of battle, particularly the Omaha Beach invasion during the Normandy landings.

LOCATIONS

The shoot began on June 27, 1997, & lasted two months. For the film, Spielberg needed a near-perfect copy of Omaha Beach, including sand and hills comparable to where German forces were stationed on that day. After extensive investigation, he discovered a close match in Ireland.

This renowned opening scene, depicting Omaha Beach in France on D-Day, was actually shot in County Wexford. Filming occurred on Ballinesker Beach, Curracloe Strand, for two months. 2,500 extras were provided by the Irish Defense Forces. The montage recreating the Omaha landings cost $12 million to produce.

Chapter Eight - TV& MOVIES

FILM RECEPTION

The film premiered July 24, 1998, and was praised by critics and moviegoers for its realism, music score, cinematography, screenplay, & direction.

The movie received numerous awards, including Golden Globes for Best Picture and Director. At the 71st Academy Awards, the film received eleven nominations and won five, including awards related to visual settings such as Best Cinematography.

BOX OFFICE

On July 24, 1998, the film was released in 2,463 theatres and made $30.5 million in its first weekend, debuting at number one and remaining there for four weeks.

The picture earned $216.5 million in the United States and Canada, and $265.3 million in other additional markets, for a total of $481.8 million worldwide. It was the highest-grossing film in the United States in 1998, and the second-highest-grossing film in the world, trailing only Armageddon. According to Box Office Mojo, Saving Private Ryan's USA & Canada ticket sales topped $45.74 million.

Chapter Eight - TV& MOVIES

PART 4 - GAME OF THRONES

HBO SMASH HIT

HBO's rendition of George R.R. Martin's books depicted a medieval

fantasy setting and came to life when shot in several locations in Northern Ireland.

LOCATIONS

The filming of Winterfell took place in Downpatrick, so you'll recognize Castle Ward from the show. As well as Theon Greyjoy near Ballintoy's small harbor.

Along with these very notable places and scenes, more filming, particularly season 1, was done for in the following places:

Paint Hall studios in Belfast

Sandy Brae in the Mourne Mountains - Exterior scenes such as Vaes Dothrak

Saintfield Estates - Winterfell Godswood

Tollymore Forest - Outdoor scenes

Cairncastle - Execution site

Magheramorne quarry - Castle Black

Shane's Castle - The Tourney Grounds

Chapter Eight - TV& MOVIES

WHY NORTHERN IRELAND?

When it came to location scouting, the producers debated shooting the bulk of the series in Scotland but ultimately chose Northern Ireland due to the availability of film studio space & generous Northern Ireland government tax breaks.

TOURIST ATTRACTIONS

Over 8 seasons and 73 episodes, the Game of Thrones drama has added not only to the Island's movie industry but has also spawned an entirely new type of tourist attraction(s) in Northern Ireland. These sights include Castle Ward in County Down to Cunshendall Caves and Ballintoy Harbour.

AWARDS

With 59 Primetime Emmy Awards, the series has won more awards than any other television drama series in history - named Outstanding Drama Series 4 times from 2015-2019. It has won 3 Hugo Awards for Top Dramatic Presentation, a Peabody, and 5 Golden Globe nominations for Best Television Series – Drama.

Chapter Eight - TV& MOVIES

PART 5 - HARRY POTTER AND THE HALF-BLOOD PRINCE

David Yates directed fantasy picture released by Warner Bros. in 2009.

The plot follows Harry as he attends Hogwarts and receives a mystery textbook, finds love, & tries to recover a memory that contains the answer to Lord Voldemort's demise.

LEMON ROCK, COUNTY KERRY

In the sixth installment of the Harry Potter film series, a single scene was creatively shot in both Kerry and Clare. In this dramatic fight scene, Dumbledore and Harry are seen standing on a solitary rock. This is Lemon Rock in County Kerry. After that, the camera swoops out over coastal rock showing the Cliffs of Moher, an iconic cliff face known around the world.

SHOOTING & COST

Shooting started on September 24, 2007, and the film was released in theatres worldwide on July 15, 2009.

At $250 million, not only is it the most expensive film to produce in the Harry Potter series, but also one of the most expensive movies made of all time.

BOX OFFICE

The film was a huge box office hit, setting the record for the highest single-day global gross. The picture grossed $394 million in five days, setting the record for the biggest five-day international gross.

AWARD NOMINATIONS

The film was nominated for Best Cinematography at the 82nd Academy Awards. The movie also received noms for Best Special Visual Effects & also Best Production Design at the 63rd British Academy Film Awards.

PART 6 - THE PRINCESS BRIDE

CLIFFS OF MOHER

The 1987 fairy-tale follows a group of knights whose mission is to save Buttercup, a beautiful princess. A masked stranger in black follows them over the water and up the Cliffs of Insanity, which are actually the stunning Cliffs of Moher of County Clare, Ireland.

The Cliffs of Moher are located in County Clare, Ireland, on the southern extremity of the Burren region. The cliffs span a distance of nearly 14 kilometers (9 miles).

CLIFF HEIGHTS

At Hag's Head, they stand 120 meters (390 feet) above the Atlantic and 8 kilometers (5 miles) north.

They reach a maximum height of 214 meters (702 feet) just north of O'Brien's Tower, a rounded stone tower at the midpoint of the cliffs built by Sir Cornelius O'Brien in 1835.

BOX OFFICE

The Rob Reiner-directed comedy, fairy-tale adventure, was considered one of the best of 1987. Although earning a modest $30.8 million at the box office ($16 million budget), it has since become a cult classic and is said to be eminently quotable.

RECEPTION

At the time of release, famed reviewers Siskel & Ebert both gave it a thumbs-up. Time said it was fun for the whole family, and the NY Times applauded the cast and crew. The film today maintains a whopping 98% Approval-rating on Rotten Tomatoes and an 8.5/10 score from listed critics. Even better is the whopping "A+" score from the audience survey on CinemaScore. Moviegoers love it.

PART 7 - VIKINGS

COUNTY WICKLOW

The picturesque County Wicklow surroundings of Luggala and the Poulaphouca Reservoir appear in the Irish-Canadian historical drama Vikings, which is set in Ireland's East.

WHY IRELAND

In July 2012, the series began production at Ireland's new Ashford (film) Studios. Primarily the scenery and additionally the tax benefits attracted the production to the Island.

ALL WICKLOW, NO GREENSCREEN

Many do not realize that the entire production of the hit show Vikings takes place in Wicklow. Shots from the History Channel episodic series have been filmed at a number of stunning Wicklow sites. The majestic valley of Luggala and the dark seas of Lough Tay, both part of the Guinness Estate, are among them. The Wicklow Mountains National

Park, south of Dublin, provides the perfect backdrop for depictions of Viking longships travel and battle. The very first season was shot outdoors for 70% of the time.

Chapter Eight - TV& MOVIES

HISTORY CHANNEL - CANADA

Michael Hirst produced and wrote the historical drama tv show Vikings for the Canadian network The History Channel. It was shot in Ireland and debuted in Canada on March 3, 2013, running for 6 seasons. This sixth season's second half was available in its entirety on Amazon Prime Video in Ireland on the 30th of December, 2020, days before its airing on The History Channel in Canada, with weekly episode drops starting January 1.

6,000,000 WATCHERS

Nielsen reports that the series premiere attracted 6 million watchers in the United States, outperforming all other broadcast networks among people aged 18 to 49.

1,000,000+ DEBUT

The debut episode drew 1.1 million viewers in Canada. The first season drew an average of 942,000 viewers each episode.

PART 8 - THE TUDORS

The Michael Hirst written historical fiction tv show The Tudors is set in 16th-century England and broadcast on the Showtime premium cable television channel. The show was created by a group of producers from the United States, the United Kingdom, and Canada and was largely shot in Ireland. Although it is centered on King Henry VIII's reign, it is titled after the entire Tudor Dynasty.

ALL IRELAND LOCATIONS

Despite its setting in England, this television drama about King Henry VIII's early years was wholly shot in Ireland. The Tudors series was filmed in Ireland at the following locations:

Christchurch Cathedral in Dublin
Powerscourt Estate, Wicklow
Ardmore Studios in Wicklow
Swords Castle in Dublin
Drimnagh Castle in Dublin

RATINGS

The Tudors began on April 1, 2007, and it quickly became Showtime's highest-rated show in three years. The show was renewed for a second season in April 2007, and the BBC announced in the same month that it had obtained worldwide rights to broadcast the series in the U.K., which it did starting on October 5, 2007. On October 2, 2007, the CBC in Canada began airing the show.

VIEWERS

The first-season debut attracted nearly 870,000 viewers in the United States. A total of 1 million people watched the première online and through cable affiliates.

AWARD NOMINATIONS

In 2007, The Tudors received a Golden Globe nomination for Best Drama Series. in addition, star Jonathan Rhys Meyers received a nomination from the Golden Globes for Best Actor in a TV Drama for his performance.

AWARDS

In 2008, the show was nominated for 8 Irish Film and TV Awards, winning seven of them, including Best Drama Series, as well as Jonathan Rhys Meyers Lead Actor, Nick Dunning for Supporting Actor, and Maria Doyle Kennedy for Supporting Actress. The show's production also won craft awards for Hair & Makeup, Production Design, and Costume Design.

REVIEWS

According to aggregate review site Metacritic, the series had 64% positive reviews in its first season, 68% in its second season, 74% in its third season, and 63% in its fourth season.

PART 9 - STAR WARS EPISODE VII: THE FORCE AWAKENS

SKELLIG MICHAEL

Star Wars, one of the biggest movie franchises in history, made quite the impact with its use of the majestic scenery that is on the West coast of Ireland. From Skellig Michael island in Kerry to Malin Head as well as the Inishowen Peninsula in Donegal's extreme north. Most notable for Ireland is the pivotal scene with Mark Hamill and Daisy Ridley, which took place over 3 days at Skellig Michael.

PLOT & BACKGROUND

J. J. Abrams produced, co-wrote, and directed this 2015 released amazing space opera picture, the 7th movie in the Skywalker Saga. The Force Awakens is set thirty years after Return of the Jedi and follows Finn, Han Solo, Rey, and Poe as they seek the whereabouts of Luke Skywalker and fight for the Resistance.

FILM BUDGET & LOCATIONS

Filming began in April 2014 on a budget of $259–306 million and ended in November 2015. The shooting took place on location in primarily Abu Dhabi, Iceland, and Ireland, as well as on stages at Pinewood (film) Studios in England.

Chapter Eight - TV& MOVIES

RELEASE

The Force Awakens opened on December 14, 2015, in Los Angeles and was released on December 18, 2015, nationwide in the USA. The screenplay, directing, and lead performances earned favorable reviews from critics.

BOX OFFICE & NOMINATIONS

The film grossed $2 billion worldwide, shattering numerous sales records and becoming the top-grossing film in the history of the United States and Canada, as well as the top-grossing film of 2015 and the third-highest-grossing movie of all time. The Academy (Awards) honored the film with 5 nominations as well as other honors at its 88th awards season.

PART 10 - RYAN'S DAUGHTER (1970)

Robert Mitchum and Sarah Miles feature in this 1970 British incredible love-drama directed by David Lean.

PLOT & LOCATIONS

Set in 1916, Ryan's Daughter depicts the story of an Irish woman who embarks on a scandalous romance with a British Soldier. The film was primarily shot on Kerry's spectacular Dingle peninsula. There is a famous scene on the beachfront between Slea Head & Dunmore Head.

BOX OFFICE & AWARDS

Critics panned Ryan's Daughter upon its debut, but the film was a box office hit, earning almost $31 million on a budget of just $13.3 million, making it the eighth-highest-grossing film of 1970. It received four Academy Award nominations and won two of them: John Miles for Best Supporting Actor and Freddie Young for Best Cinematography....some say easy with such a beautiful Irish setting.

REVIEWS

Many film critics were harsh in their reviews of Ryan's Daughter when it first came out. It received two out of four stars from Roger Ebert, 1.5 stars from his co-host Gene Siskel, and a "brilliant enigma" from Variety.

Chapter Eight - TV& MOVIES

1916 EASTER RISING

The film was also chastised for its portrayal of the Irish proletariat as primitive and barbaric. Some saw the film as an attempt to discredit and alter the memory of the 1916 Easter Rising and subsequent Irish War of Independence, particularly in light of the outbreak of "the Troubles" in Northern Ireland near its time of release.

MASTERPIECE

Some critics have re-evaluated Ryan's Daughter since its DVD release in recent years, with some calling it an underappreciated masterpiece.

PART 11 - RANDOM FAST FACTS #4

IRISH AMERICAN PRESIDENTS
According to some historians, more than 40% of all U.S. Presidents have Irish heritage.

TALL TWINS
The Knipe Brothers, born in 1761 in Magherafelt, County Derry, were the world's tallest identical twins, standing at 2.2 meters or 7ft 2 in height.

IRISH DIALECTS
Ulster, Connacht, and Munster are the three major dialects of Irish spoken today. The vocabulary, grammar, and pronunciation of each dialect vary slightly.

WOMAN'S CHRISTMAS
In Irish, January 6 is known as "Nollaig na mBan" - Women's Christmas.

BUTTER
County Cork was the world's top exporter of butter in the late 1700s, mainly to the UK.

YACHT CLUB
The Royal Cork Yacht Club is the world's oldest yacht club (fd. 1720)

CORK HARBOUR

Cork Harbour claims to be the world's second-largest natural harbor, 54 sq km or nearly 21 sq miles behind Sydney Australia's Port Jackson, 55 sq km or 21 sq miles.

UNION JACK

On the 1st of January 1801 in Dublin, the Union Jack was hoisted for the first time, symbolizing the union of Great Britain and Ireland.

SCOTLAND PROXIMITY

Northern Ireland is barely 13 miles away from Scotland's coast at its closest point.

JFK, SHAMROCKS & GREEN TIE

Ireland's ambassador to the United States, Thomas Kiernan, arrived at the White House with a bowl of shamrock on March 17, 1963. JFK, 35th President of the United States of America, donned a green tie for photographs.

MOBILE PHONES

There is an est. 4M active mobile phone in Ireland as of 2022. An increase of 600,000 since 2018. Ireland's total pop. = 4.9M

LONG LEASE

Arthur Guinness, the famous brewer, leased the land for his brewery for 9,000 years, starting in 1759.

LEGAL DIVORCE

The very first legal divorce in Ireland occurred on January 17, 1997.

chapter nine
FOOD, TEA, TOBACCO

PART 1 - POTATOES

It's cliche, but most Irish people really do enjoy a good potato.

It's interesting to note that the Irish potato we recognize and love today isn't even Irish! The traditional white potato comes from South America.

The starchy food is adored in all shapes, sizes, and forms. Whether boiling, roasting, mashing, making Champ with milk, butter, and spring onions, or frying into Boxty are all delicious options.

FLUFFY MASHED AND CARROTS

Mashed potato, sweet potato, and/or even turnip with carrot and rutabaga. Top with caramelized onions.

BANGERS AND MASH

Not just for the English. Cheap, filling, and any variety of sausage for this potato and meat dish, topped with savory onion gravy. Cook the sausage too quickly, and they'll go "bang."

DUBLIN POTATO CODDLE

Hearty stewed meal is a favorite in its namesake city. Potatoes, bacon, carrots, and sausage with beef stock or with chicken if one prefers a lighter flavor.

SHEPHERD'S PIE

This tasty dish must be made with lamb, a favored meat in Ireland, or it is actually "cottage pie." Ground or minced lamb will suffice.

TRADITIONAL COLCANNON

A British Isle signature dish of potatoes and cabbage. This starchy, hearty side dish was said to be made in 1875 but likely a lot longer ago. Many add bacon and chopped herbs. The same recipe without cabbage is called "Irish Champ."

NORTHUMBERLAND PAN HAGGERTY

AKA Potato casserole. Eaten in regular rotation alongside sausage, this cheddar topped meal is not just popular and claimed by the English, but that of the Irish.

TRADITIONAL POTATOES O'BRIEN

Traditional dish that makes use of your leftover potatoes. Boiled or baked with added cheese, peppers, and garlic make this the ultimate comfort food. Add in a protein of sorts, and you have a version of (corned beef) hash. Often served with eggs and sausage, or a side at dinner.

IRISH POTATO PANCAKES

AKA "Boxty" is the Irish latkes. Made with leftover and sometimes freshly-finely grated potato is cooked evenly at low heat and dusted with powdered sugar. Serve with butter and applesauce.

TRADITIONAL BUBBLE & SQUEAK

From the sound of cooking cabbage & beef over a fire as it "bubbled & squeaked away."

An Irish (& British) breakfast of any leftover veg (not just cabbage) and mash, beef if available. Top it with a fried egg for a heavy breakfast or brunch.

PART 2 - STEW & VEGETABLE SOUP

If you've ever been to Ireland, you'll know that the land of leprechauns isn't always blessed with mild, dry, or the warmest of temperatures. Therefore, the locals like to cook up warm, hearty meals.

HELLO, IRISH STEW!

This traditional Irish recipe includes tossing a lot of ingredients into a large pot and letting it "stew" for many hours until serving.

Carrots, Parsley, Onions, of course, potatoes, and then some varieties of meat are among the ingredients that vary depending on personal choice and recipe.

Locals will debate saying any veg and any meat on hand stewed right is an Irishman's delight. Perfect for a chilly, rainy winter evening!

VEGETABLE SOUP

Vegetable Soup, like Irish Stew, is a fantastic dish for a cold winter night, and it's still very wildly popular today.

A traditional vegetable soup mix includes potatoes, barley, carrots, lentils, celery, leeks, peas, and in some cases, even meat.

PART 3 - FISH

Living on a small island, fishing and fish becomes a way of life. The Irish enjoy fresh seafood like no other: Dublin Bay prawns, Wild salmon, and fresh oysters are just some of the islander's favorites.

SMOKED MACKEREL FISHCAKES

Smoked fish meals tend to be economical but flavorful. These fishcakes make use of hard-boiled eggs with added horseradish cream for richness and zest. Splashed with lemon, these are seen as a full meal or

welcomed side-dish on many, many Irish tables. Fried 3min a side and best served hot on a bed of veg/pea puree.

AKA FISHCAKES - AMERICANS

An American eater may be more familiar with the fishcake/tuna fishcake/tuna cake version - mashed potato, tuna, herbs, possible onion

in a patty form, may be baked or fried (fried is recommended)

SIMPLE TRADITIONAL FISH PIE

Seafood version of a cottage (not shepherd's) pie. This lower-cost, all-in-one meal is made with fish scraps rather than whole cuts and is best topped with fluffy mashed potato.

PART 4 - BREAD AS POPULAR AS POTATOES

The Irish are not only known for their love of potatoes, but also their love of bread. Popular types include:

SODA FARLS
Farl, meaning 4. Cutting a flatbread round of dough into 4 parts, then baking. Cut and served warm from the oven with room temperature spreads.

WHEATEN BREAD
AKA "brown soda bread" has a very thick, dense dough thanks to the mixed-in buttermilk. Often made with wholemeal mixed with white and zapped rolled oats.

FADGE
AKA Potato Bread AKA Scottish Tattie Scones. With or without egg, though that gives it lightness, these scones or Tattie Scones use leftover mash. Serve them with butter, clotted cream, or jam for the morning meal.

SODA BREAD
In Ireland, this sodium bicarbonate (baking soda) bread is made with white or whole wheat flour and most times served toasted, spread with salted Irish butter.

POTATO BREAD (OF COURSE)
Potatoes, bread, stews, fish cakes, and more. Ireland does indeed have its own 'flavor.'

PART 5 - TEA

CONSUMPTION

Ireland is the #2 per capita tea consumer in the world. The Emerald Isle drinks 2.2kg or 4.38lb per person per year.

In contrast, the #1 country for most tea-drinking per capita is Turkey, with 3.2kg or 7lb per person per year.

Iran is #3 with 2kg or 4.4lb, the UK is 4th with 1.5kg or 3.3lb per year, and Russia comes in at #4 with 1.4kg or 3.1lb. The USA is way back at #35, consuming .23kg or .5lb.

3 IN 4 ARE REGULAR DRINKERS

Sources claim 3 in 4 people of Ireland are regular tea drinkers.

CUPS PER DAY

The average person drinks between 4 and 6 cups a day.

WHAT'S IN THE CUP

Most prefer their tea with 2 sugars and a 1/4 to a 1/3 cup of milk.

TOP BRANDS

The top brands are Barry's Tea, followed by Lyon's Tea, and next is Bewley's Tea. Many Irish say it is just the top 2, like the battle between colas Coke and Pepsi.

Chapter Nine - FOOD, TEA, TOBACCO

BARRY'S
Barry's is a blend of East Africa teas and became a national brand in the 1960s.

LYON'S
Established in Dublin in 1902, Lyon's is a blend of Kenyan and Indonesian teas.

BEWLEY'S
Bewley's, now based in Dublin, sprang up from tea imported directly from China starting in 1835.

BLACK
Black tea dominates the taste buds year after year.

FINGER FOODS
Irish treats to enjoy with tea include scones, chocolate potato cake, cucumber sandwiches with cream cheese, and sausage rolls. Also, bite-sized sandwiches like Marmite and watercress, meat with Branston pickles, and Hobnob brand biscuits.

THREE RECOGNIZED TEA TIMES INCLUDE
11:00 AM AKA Elevenses. Served with scones and biscuits (don't call them cookies).

3:00 - 5:00 PM AKA Afternoon Tea. Served with light sweet items.

6:00 PM AKA High Tea. Referred to as dinner or supper depending on the region. More popular in the north and serves food of substance including fruit, bread, meat, fish, and Irish cheese.

PART 6 - TOBACCO

WORLDWIDE

Cigarettes were used by over 1 billion individuals in 2014, or approximately 20% of the world's population over the age of 15.

Tobacco use is on the decline in developed nations, but on the rise in the undeveloped, particularly among males.

IRELAND

Ireland is 96th in the world for tobacco consumption. 26% of Irish males and 21% of females of 15 years+ are regular smokers. This is a significant decline since 2000 when 34% of males and 36% of females were regular smokers, a drop of 8% and 15% respectively.

AREAS THAT SMOKE

Smoking is more prevalent in Ireland's rural areas than in cities

COUNTRY WITH THE MOST SMOKERS

The country with a significant population with the highest % of smokers is Myanmar in SE Asia. With 55 million people, 70% of males & 21% of females, or nearly 46% of all citizens over 15 years of age, are regular smokers.

CHINA - PRODUCTION

China produces and consumes approximately 30% of the global tobacco

AMERICA

Smoking in America is on the decline, dropping by 1/2 from 1965-2006, or 42% to 21%, continuing the trend down to 14% as of 2018

PART 7 - RANDOM FAST FACTS #5

LOW DIVORCE RATE

After more than 25 years of legal divorce, Ireland has the 4-lowest divorce rate in the world.

THOUSANDS OF CASTLES

It is estimated that Ireland has over 25,000 castles and ruins spread out across the island. Tourists are welcome to stay in several of the castles.

CHURCH ATTENDANCE

Ireland has one of the greatest church attendance rates in Europe, with over 80% of the population = Roman Catholic.

GUILLOTINE

The guillotine was first used in Ireland in 1307, predating France's first use in 1792

BOYCOTT IS IRISH

The term "boycott" was coined in the Irish county of Mayo. Charles Cunningham Boycott, an English land dealer, contributed the verb "to boycott" to the English language after being shunned by his Irish community.

Chapter Nine - FOOD, TEA, TOBACCO

MOVIE – "THE QUIET MAN"
Cong, Co. Mayo was the setting for the iconic Irish film "The Quiet Man." Each year, more than 40,000 tourists go to Cong to soak in the sights and sounds of the renowned film.

U2
Bono, the Edge, and their band U2 formed in Dublin in 1976. Their earliest taste of success came in 1978, winning a talent contest in Limerick on St. Patrick's Day.

ZINC MINE
The Tara Mine, located near Navan in County Meath, is Europe's largest zinc mine and the world's sixth-largest.

WINDMILLS = CLOCKWISE
Windmills in Ireland are the only windmills in the world that rotate clockwise. It is entirely dependent on the windmill's motor, but in general, more Ireland windmills are configured to turn clockwise than in other countries.

TALK SHOW
The Late Late Show (July 1962 - present) is a talk show broadcast from Ireland. After The Tonight Show (Sept. 1954) in the United States, it is the world's second-longest-running late-night talk show.

STIFF DRINKS
In Ireland, a 'Standard Drink' contains 25% more alcohol than in the U.K.

chapter ten

LANGUAGE, SLANG, JOKES

Chapter Ten - LANGUAGE, SLANG, JOKES

PART 1 - GAELIC

Irish Gaelic, or simply "Gaelic," is the native language of the Irish people. This Goidelic language of the insular Celtic part of the broader family of Celtic languages was Ireland's 1st language until the late 1700s.

EDUCATION
Because of the educational system, 1.7 million or 40% of people profess to be proficient in Irish, but only 380,000 (some say 73,000) people are genuine, regular native speakers.

GAELIC SPEAKING AREAS
The areas (counties) of Kerry, Donegal, Cork, Galway still speak Irish Gaelic as a 1st language. Smaller areas such as Waterford, Meath, and Mayo also have many Gaelic (primary) speakers.

SCOTTISH GAELIC & MANX
The Irish people spread their Gaelic language into Scotland with Scottish Gaelic and Manx, but also to countries such as Canada with 250,000 daily speakers in the Great White North back in 1890.

Chapter Ten - LANGUAGE, SLANG, JOKES

PART 2 - ENGLISH WORDS INTO IRISH

HELLO
There is no one way or exact way to say "Hello."

"Dia Duit" pronounced ("jee-ah-gwit") in English means "God be with you", formal sense.

"Cad é mar atá tú?" pronounced ("ka-JAY mar uh-TAH too") is a common greeting, in English meaning "How are You?"

GOODBYE
"Slán" pronounced ("Slawn") is the most common form of goodbye, a parting-way greeting.

Slán abhaile pronounced ("slawn a-wal-ya") is used to bid goodbye to someone that is traveling (back) home. In English, it translates to "safe home"; abhaile means "homeward."

I LOVE YOU
"Tá mo chroí istigh ionat" pronounced ("taw mu kree iss-chig un-it") is an expression of love that translates to English as "my heart of within you" or more casually accepted is "my heart is in you."

BEAUTIFUL
"Galánta" is pronounced ("galaanta") in English, meaning elegant, attractive, charming, or simply beautiful. This can be used to describe a person or informally the weather.

Chapter Ten - LANGUAGE, SLANG, JOKES

GOOD LUCK

"Ádh Mór" pronounced ("aw mór") in English means good luck.

An extension is Ádh mór (ort), pronounced (AW MORE (OH-rut)) in English means "Good luck (to you)."

"Go n-éirí leat" pronounced (guh NIGH-rhee LAT) also implies luck but translates to "May you succeed."

CHEERS

"Sláinte" pronounced ("slawn-che") in English means "health." A derivative of sláinte is "sláinte is táinte" pronounced ("slawn-che iss toin-che"), in English means "health and wealth."

YES

"Sea," a short form of "is ea" or "it is," and is acceptable for a simple, informal "yes."

"tá" is a formal use of "yes" for such usage as, e.g., on an election card.

"Táim" pronounced ("thaw-im") is not translated directly to "yes" but is actually "I am." So if asked the question "Are you going to work?" one would answer "Táim" or the abbreviated "Tá mé" meaning "I am." Or contextually, "Sea, bím" means "Yes, I do be"

NO

"Ni-hea" is acceptable for a simple, informal "no."

"Níl" is a formal use of "no" for such usage as for, e.g., an election card.

IRISH

"Éireannach" or "Éireann" for short and in adjective form.

"Gaeilge" is used when referring to the language, which easily resembles "Gaelic."

FRIEND

"Cara" pronounced ("keer + a") is an acceptable Irish word for friend.

LOVE

"Grá" pronounced ("graw") is an acceptable form of the English word "love" in an affectionate way but not exotic or erotic love. It can be used informally in conversation to communicate endearment.

"Grádh" is an older, considered obsolete usage, Scottish.

THANK YOU

"Go raibh maith agat" pronounced ("gur-uv mah ah-guth") is a common expression of gratitude translating to "thank you" or "good thank you" in English.

PART 3 - COUNTY SLANG

The Irish are not known to hold their tongue, can be forward, and sometimes down-right mean about it. Whether you are cheap, dense, careless, or even unattractive, there's a saying for it. Oh, and there are a few compliments, or some that can be perceived as compliments sprinkled into the mix.

Each Ireland & Northern Ireland County (32) has their own slang. Here is one from each

ANTRIM – "DOUBLE-BAGGER"
Means: He or she is attractive: They cover up their ugliness with a paper bag over the head, and you cover your head in shame for being with them

ARMAGH –" TAKE HER HANDY"
Means: Be careful, take care.

CARLOW – "HE RAN LIKE DA CLAPPERS"
Means: He ran away at a fast pace

CAVAN – "YER SOME BOY, YOU ARE"
Means: You're an idiot, clown

Chapter Ten - LANGUAGE, SLANG, JOKES

CLARE – "STALL THE DIGGER"
Means: Stop what you are doing -or- Take it easy

CORK – "YOU HAD A HILO"
Means: You had an accident -or- you had a fall

DERRY – "TAKE A LOOK AT THE SHAPE OF HIM (OR HER)"
Means: Look at how that person's actions -or- how they dress

DONEGAL – "LIKE A BAG O' WEASELS"
Means: Describes a person in a bad mood -or- a person who is difficult to talk to.

DOWN – "SNARED A WAKER"
Means: Caught out-right doing something that you shouldn't have.

DUBLIN – "D'YA KNOW WAH I MEAN, LIKE?"
Means: "Do you understand what I am trying to tell you?" Many times ending an incoherent statement.

GALWAY – "I'VE SEEN BETTER MEN ON TOP OF WEDDING CAKES"
Means: Describes an unattractive man -or- a man with a more attractive girlfriend, spouse

KILKENNY – "YA COMING FOR A PUCK ABOUT?"
Means: Are you coming to play a light game/short time of hurling?

Chapter Ten - LANGUAGE, SLANG, JOKES

FERMANAGH – "THERE'S A WANT IN YA AS BIG AS AN ASS"

Means: Describes a stupid or not-so-sharp person

KERRY – "ARE YA PICKING UP WHAT I'M PUTTING DOWN?"

Means: Do you understand what I am saying?

KILDARE – "ALRIGHT LID, ANY STIR?"

Means: Lid = Kildare County pronunciation of Lad, and "any stir" means "what's up"

LAOIS – "THAT FELLA IS AS FECKIN' MANE"

Means: Cheap, never reaches into their pocket to pay

LEITRIM – "'MON WE GET LANGERS"

Means: Come with me, we are going to get very drunk

LIMERICK – "ACTING THE MAGGOT"

Means: Lighthearted insult, when someone is joking -or- when someone is up to no good.

ROSCOMMON – "TIGHT AS A DUCK'S ARSE"
Means: Known to be cheap or excessively frugal, will not spend money.

SLIGO – "I HAVEN'T GOT A BALLS NOTION"
Means: Someone admitting they are completely, utterly clueless about the subject

LONGFORD – "THAT FELLA WOULD ROB THE MILK OUT OF YOUR TEA"
Means: A person with no morals, they'll steal anything

LOUTH – "THE SHAPE OF YA"
Means: An insult towards someone's physical appearance, often part of many insults

MAYO – "CHILL THE BEANS"
Means: Someone wants you to calm down and relax.

MEATH – "CHANCE YOUR ARM AT IT"
Means: You may as well try anything, because what is the worst that could happen?

MONAGHAN – "CHANCIN' QUARE ONES"
Means: You are so desperate for a mate that you are trying girls/guys of a lower standard than normal

OFFALY – "AWAY WITH THE FAIRIES"
Means: Someone in a world of their own, detached from the present situation.

Chapter Ten - LANGUAGE, SLANG, JOKES

TIPPERARY – "HAVING A RIGHT SHNEERE"
Means: You are having a great time, together, likely with laughs

TYRONE – "A DAY FOR THE HAY"
Means: Currently experiencing good weather, ideal for farming.

WATERFORD – "YOU'RE ABOUT AS USEFUL AS A KILKENNY MAN WITH A FOOTBALL"
Means: Implying you are useless, bad at the task on hand

WESTMEATH – "TELL YOUR STORY WALKING"
Means: They have no interest in what you have to say; they want you to walk away as you speak it.

WEXFORD – "THE SMELL OF RAGE OFF YA"
When you sense someone's angry by their physical movement(s)

WICKLOW – "THAT'LL LEARN HIM"
Means: That will (surely) teach him a lesson

(CREDIT: irelandbeforeyoudie.com)

PART 4 - IRISH JOKES

Q: How can you tell if a shamrock is jealous?

A: Because it will be GREEN with envy.

Q: Why should you never iron a 4-leaf clover?

A: Because you do not want to press your luck

Q: What might a ghost drink on St. Patrick's Day?

A: BOOs

Q: Why does one wear a shamrock on St. Patrick's Day?

A: Because a regular rock is just too heavy.

Q: What do you call a criminal leprechaun?

A: A lepre-con.

Q: How are a 4-leaf clover and good friend alike?

A: They're both hard to find.

Chapter Ten - LANGUAGE, SLANG, JOKES

Q: What do you call leprechauns who collect bottles, cans, and old newspapers?

Wee-cyclers.

Q: What is wrestler and actor Dwayne Johnson's Irish name?

A: Sham-ROCK

Q: Why are the Irish so worried about climate change?

A: Because they're really into green living.

Man: I met an Irishman in County Cavan.

Woman: Oh, really?

Man: No, O'Reilly

Q: What do you hear when 2 leprechauns converse?

A: A lot of small talk.

Chapter Ten - LANGUAGE, SLANG, JOKES

Q: What's green, long, and appears 1x a year?

A: St. Patrick's Day parade.

Q: When does the leprechaun cross the road?

A: When the light turns green.

Q: What happens when you combine poison ivy and a 4-leaf clover?

A: A rash of good luck

Q: Why can't you borrow any money from a leprechaun?

A: Because they are always much too short.

Q: How can you tell an Irishman loves your joke?

A: Because he's 'Dublin' over with laughter.

Chapter Ten - LANGUAGE, SLANG, JOKES

Q: What's an Irishman's favorite music?

A: Sham-ROCK

Q: Where can an Irishman always find a shamrock?

A: In the dictionary, of course.

Q: Why are the Irish sooooo cheap?

They refuse to give up the green.

(CREDIT: irelandbeforeyoudie.com)

PART 5 - IRELAND SLANG

"Black Stuff" - Guinness

"Blottoed" - Falling over drunk

"Slammers" - Drunk off one's 'arse'

"Shift" - (to) French kiss

"Craic" (pronounced "crack") - To have a good time, conversation

"Deadly" - Cool, Very good, awesome

"Langered" - (He/They are) drunk

"Kingding" or "Kanye West" - Egotistical, Thinks highly of themselves

"Off your nut" - Drunk

"Short" - A shot of hard liquor

"Dingwop" - Dumb, stupid person

"Scoop" - Alcoholic Beverage

"Class" - Of good quality (e.g., a beer)

(CREDIT: irisharoundtheworld.com)

PART 6 - RANDOM FAST FACTS #6

RED LIGHT
Montgomery Street in Dublin used to be Europe's largest red-light district.

PHOENIX PARK
Phoenix Park (1,750-acre city park) in Dublin is double the size of Central Park, NYC (843 acres).

GAMBLING
In Ireland, sports betting is legal.

POLISH SPEAKERS
Recent census shows more Polish speakers in Ireland than native speakers of Gaelic, Ireland's indigenous language.

POSTAL
Ireland was the European Union's final country to lack a postal code system (intro'd 2014).

DUNDALK JAIL
The famous Dundalk Jail was designed in 1853 by a Dundalk citizen named John Neville. Legend has it he was its first occupant (bankruptcy).

Chapter Ten - LANGUAGE, SLANG, JOKES

BIKES
In April 2016, 56,837 citizens rode their bikes to work, up 43% from 2011.

CONTRACEPTIVES
Until 1985, a prescription was required in order to purchase condoms in Ireland.

TREE FAIRIES
A road in Ireland had building postponed for ten years before being relocated to protect a tree considered home to fairies.

LARGEST COUNTY
County Cork is Ireland's largest county by area, with 7,457 q km or 2,879 sq miles.

PUBS IN CORK
There is 1 pub for every 500 persons in Co. Cork, Ireland.

WICKLOW - NICKNAME
The people of Wicklow are known as 'goat suckers' because of the goats that roamed the Wicklow mountains.

NO SMOKING
In 2004, Ireland became the first country to impose a complete ban on smoking in the workplace, in pubs, and in restaurants across the entire country.

BALL FOR NYE IN NYC
Ireland's Waterford Crystal manufactures the ball dropped in NYC's Times Square on New Year's Eve.

chapter eleven
SPORTS

Chapter Eleven - SPORTS

PART 1 - SPORTS

OVER 50% PARTICIPATION

In Irish culture, sport plays a significant part, and its impact is seen in every Irish village as well as in every town and city. Not only do the Irish support by watching their local/national teams but over half of Ireland's population themselves participates in sporting events at least one time a week.

SPORTS PLAYED & WATCHED

Popular sports include Football (Soccer), Rugby, Cricket, Hurling. Gaelic Football, Boxing – Combat Sports, Racing and Golf. Each sport has its superstars with many gaining fame on the world stage for their accomplishments and media presence.

#1 SPORT(S)

Although football (soccer) is thought to be the #1 sport participated in and enjoyed, attending the top prize actually goes to the collective of Gaelic Games.

PART 2 - GAELIC GAMES

OFFICIAL #1

Gaelic Games officially eclipsed football (soccer) as Ireland's most popular sport for the first time in nine years, according to research from the 2018 (TSSI) Teneo Sport and Sponsorship Index.

GAELIC GAME SPORTS

Gaelic Games have a long history in Ireland and are the country's own indigenous sports. Gaelic Football, Hurling, Camogie, and Handball are the four sports that make up Gaelic games.

OLDEST SPORT

Hurling is the oldest sport in Ireland, dating back thousands of years. With over 2,200 GAA clubs in Ireland, these games are deeply rooted in nearly every Ireland town and play a vital role in the lives of Irish people.

PART 3 - GAELIC FOOTBALL

FIRST PLAYED
Most Popular isn't Football (soccer) but that of Gaelic Games, notably Gaelic Football, a team sport created by the Irish and first played in 1885.

FIELD & PLAYERS
It is played on a rectangular grass surface involving two teams of 15 players each.

HOW IS IT PLAYED?
Much like a hybrid of football (soccer) and rugby, the purpose of the game is to kick or punch the ball into the goals of the opposing side.

Players can advance by kicking, passing, or bouncing the ball, with the two kinds of scoring having distinct values: net goals are worth three points, while a kick through the uprights is worth one point.

NON-PROFESSIONAL
The sport is a part of the Gaelic Games, which also includes Hurling, Camogie, and Handball. Despite being the most popular sport in Ireland, it remains an amateur sport.

Gaelic Football is one of the rare sports in which neither the players, coaches, organizations, nor staff earn pay or any other sort of compensation.

PART 4 - HURLING

OLDEST SPORT
Hurling is another indigenous Irish sport with a centuries-old history, some say to ancient times.

HOW IS IT PLAYED?
It is played between two 15-player teams, each with a hurl, which is a wooden club with a scooped head. Players pass a little ball to each other and attempt to score by hitting it into a goal.

LIKE LACROSSE
It's similar to lacrosse, except that instead of catching the ball with your club and then throwing it, you catch it and then hit it.

LIKE BASKETBALL
It also bears some resemblance to basketball. For instance, you can only carry the ball four steps before passing it.

NOT JUST IN IRELAND
Hurling is a Gaelic sport and considered a part of Irish culture. Leagues also exist in the United States, Canada, New Zealand, Argentina, Australia, Europe, South Africa, and South Korea.

PART 5 - BOXING / COMBAT SPORTS

Many sources claim that combat sports and boxing are gaining more popularity in Ireland faster than any other sport in modern times.

BOXING SUCCESS AT THE OLYMPIC LEVEL

The country has competed in boxing at the Olympics on a regular basis, with several of its boxers' winning medals. Irish boxers won seven medals, including one gold at both the 2008 and 2012 Olympic Games.

MMA – CONOR MCGREGOR

Along with boxing, athletes like Conor McGregor have helped to boost the appeal of combat sports in Ireland to heights never seen before. A former 2-weight division champion with the world's largest promotion, McGregor's stardom has earned him the #1, or one of the highest-paid of all sports athletes in 2021

BOXING & MMA GYMS

And it's not just professionals and Olympians participating. Boxing and MMA gyms are also growing in popularity, with new clubs and training centers springing up all across the country on a regular basis.

PART 6 - FOOTBALL (SOCCER)

MEN'S NATIONAL TEAM

Football, Futbol or Soccer as it is known in other parts of the world, is by far the most popular sport on the earth and a long-time favorite of the Irish.

At the highest level of the sport is the Men's National Team, which is currently ranked 47th in the world, while the women's National squad is ranked 31st.

MEN'S MONIKER

Nicknamed "The Boys in Green" or "Jack's Army," the men's team has been ranked as low as 70th (2014) and as high as 6th (1993) in international play.

MEN'S OLYMPIC SUCCESS

The 1924 Olympics was the national team's debut and reached quarter-final play.

MEN'S FIFA SUCCESS

The team has appeared in the FIFA World Cup 3 times, the first appearance being 1990 and that year made it to the Quarter-finals. The team also made the UEFA European Championship tournament 3 times, doing so first in 1988 and making that year's Final 8.

Chapter Eleven - SPORTS

The National team's longest competitive win streak came in 1989 for 1990 World Cup qualifying, where the team strung together 5 consecutive victories.

MEN'S BEST FINISHES

Although no top finish at the Olympics, or World Cup, Ireland has achieved 1st place in 2 competitions: Winners of the 1986 Iceland Triangular Tournament, a 3-team competition played in Iceland between Iceland, Czechoslovakia,  and The Republic of Ireland. Also, 1st place in the 2011 Celtic Nations Cup, a 4-team tournament between Wales, Northern Ireland, Scotland, and the Republic of Ireland.

MEN'S TOP PLAYER

Robbie Keane (1998-2016) is Ireland's all-time top goal-scorer (68) and the most capped (146).

WOMEN'S NATIONAL TEAM

Despite numerous attempts at Invitational competitions such as the Algarve Cup, the Istria Cup, and the Cyprus Cup, the Republic of Ireland women's team has yet to qualify for an event.

Chapter Eleven - SPORTS

WOMEN'S MONIKER

In 1973 the team nicknamed "The Girls in Green" came to be securing their first win, 3-2 vs. Wales in a Friendly match. In 1982 they played in their first competitive match, losing to Scotland in a Euro qualifier, but gained their first victory this time over Northern Ireland 2-1 in the same qualifying tourney.

WOMEN'S BEST FINISH

The best finish for the women's squad was #1 - winning the 4-team Celt Cup in 2000 over teams from Northern Ireland, Scotland, and the Isle of Man.

WOMEN'S BIGGEST WIN

Just recently, the team's biggest win ever came in November 2021, when they defeated Georgia 11–0 in the World Cup qualifiers for 2023.

WOMEN'S TOP PLAYERS

Emma Byrne (1996-2017) has the most Caps (134)

Olivia O'Toole (1991-2009) has the most goals scored (54)

PART 7 - GOLF

IRELAND'S TOP PLAYERS

Golf has long been a popular sport throughout Europe, and Ireland is no exception. Ireland has produced some of the most well-known golfers in history, including Shane Lowrie, Peter Lawrie, and Harrington.

NORTHERN IRELAND'S MCIIROY

Rory McIlroy is Northern Ireland's top golfer. He is part of the PGA TOUR and the European Tour. He is a 4-time major champion and spent more than 100 weeks as golf's top-rated player.

IRELAND COURSES & COMPETITIONS

Ireland is home to some of the best courses in the world, with a number of them frequently ranking in the top 100 in Europe and worldwide.

There are 300 golf courses on the island, with numerous link-style courses along the shore.

Several events are held in both Ireland and Northern Ireland throughout the year, including amateur and women's tournaments, as well as the Irish Open.

PART 8 - RUGBY

Gaelic football may be more popular, but rugby is still played regularly in Ireland, from schoolboy to professional levels.

IRISH NATIONAL TEAM
The Irish national team, unlike football (soccer) teams, is made up of players from both Ireland and Northern Ireland.

NATIONAL TEAM'S #1
The national team has been ranked number one in the globe for the first time in 2019 and dates back to 1875.

TOP PLAYERS
Ireland has produced some of rugby's most famous players, with a handful being voted into the Hall of Fame.

Ronan O'Gara and Brian O'Driscoll are two of the most well-known figures in the sport in Ireland.

WORLD CUP

Ireland, like some other rugby-playing nations, has a Sevens team that competes in tournaments, including the World Cup.

SIX NATIONS COMPETITION

Ireland has had a great deal of success on the rugby world stage in recent years, defeating the dominating All Blacks multiple times, earning two Six Nations titles in 2014 but also 2015, and a fantastic Grand Slam in 2018.

POPULARITY

These sporting achievements have contributed to the growth of the sport's appeal in Ireland, with the Aviva Stadium often drawing sold-out crowds.

PART 9 - CRICKET

England may be more renowned for cricket, but Ireland has been steadily improving and increasing the popularity of the sport in its own right.

ICC MEMBERSHIP

Ireland was an associate member of the ICC until 2017 when it was joined by Afghanistan as a full member.

Cricket is less well-known in Ireland than some of the other international famed sports. Ireland's full ICC status, on the other hand, allows it to compete in high-profile contests against major opponents such as India, New Zealand, and Australia.

QUALIFICATIONS

Ireland competes in all three forms of cricket: (ODIs) One-Day Internationals, Test Matches, and (T20s) Twenty20 matches. They frequently must qualify for larger competitions, including World Cups, by playing teams such as Afghanistan, Scotland, and Namibia.

PART 10 - RANDOM FAST FACTS #7

WOODENBRIDGE HOTEL
Opening its doors in 1608, the Woodenbridge Hotel is the oldest hotel in Ireland.

HOSPITAL
Hospital is the name of a village in Limerick, Ireland. Ironically it lacks a hospital.

UFO
The Irish have Europe's least number of UFO sightings.

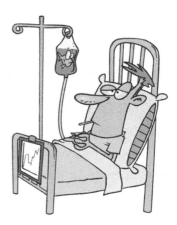

LEAST RAIN
In Ireland, May is typically the driest month of the year.

LOTTERY WINNERS
A group of 16 players from a concrete business in County Carlow won the highest Irish Lottery jackpot worth €18,963,441 ($21,147,000 USD).

INVENTIONS
Rubber-soled shoes, Whiskey distillation, Portable defibrillator, Colour photography, Flavoured Crisps, are all Ireland inventions.

SYRINGES
Francis Rynd, an Irishman, devised the hollow needle for syringes in 1844.

OSCAR DESIGN IS IRISH
Cedric Gibbons, an Irishman, designed the Oscar statue in 1928.

ROTUNDA HOSPITAL
The Rotunda Hospital in Dublin, first opened in 1745, is the world's oldest continually operating maternity hospital.

MORE INVENTIONS
Ejector Seat, TransAtlantic Calls, Guided Missile, Tank, Guinness, Modern Tractor, and Hypodermic Syringe are all Ireland inventions.

BLARNEY STONE
The 'Gift of the Gab' is claimed to be bestowed upon those who kiss Blarney's famous parapet stone.

DOGS
Irish Wolfhounds are the world's tallest dog breed.

SHORTEST PARADE
The official route for the World's Shortest St. Patrick's Day Parade is just 98 feet long (Hot Springs, Arkansas).

CLOSED ON ST. PADDY'S DAY
As a symbol of respect for this religious day, until 1970, Irish law prevented pubs from operating on St. Patrick's Day, March 17.

chapter twelve
ATHLETES

Chapter Twelve - ATHLETES

PART 1 - ROY KEAN - FOOTBALL (SOCCER) MIDFIELDER (B. 1971)

A former professional footballer from Ireland who now has managed the Irish national team and various clubs as well as worked in the booth.

GREATEST OF ALL TIME

Kean is arguably the most accomplished Irish footballer of all time, with 19 major trophies to his name in his club career, 17 while playing for Manchester United in England. He was featured in Pelé's FIFA 100 list of the world's finest living players in 2004; as a top midfielder of his generation. He was voted No. 11 on the list of the 50 hardest-footballers of all time in 2007 by The Times. He was known for his gruff and arrogant demeanor. In 2021, Keane was elected into the Premier League Hall-of-Fame.

THE FEROCIOUS ONE

At one time the core of Ireland's and Manchester United's midfield. Tough as nails and not one to put up with idiots, slackers, or softies, Keane's unrelenting quest of excellence on the pitch was both his biggest attribute – and his worst flaw. Keane's flawless standard-setting resulted in many ugly, expletive-filled bust-ups with Mick McCarthy. Keane's technical ability is sometimes forgotten among the cartoon portrayals of the hot-headed rugged man. He was a tremendously effective playmaker as well as a killer in the middle of the park, in his own unflashy way.

PART 2 - LIAM BRADY – FOOTBALL (SOCCER) MIDFIELDER (B. 1956)

PLAYMAKER EXTRAORDINAIRE

One of the best playmakers in history and maybe the most creative player to ever emerge from the great nation of Ireland. The Arsenal midfielder boasted a left foot of exceptional quality. His refined abilities were also recognized in Italy, where he played for the famous Juventus and Inter Milan clubs during the 1980s.

NO INTERNATIONAL PLAY

Unfortunately, 'Chippy' Brady (nicknamed for his fondness of chips) never competed in a major international competition. Brady's Ireland narrowly missed out on qualification for the 1982 World Cup finals to France, and when the Boys in Green qualified for Euro 88, Brady – who was then in the midst of his West Ham career – was intentionally (some say) left off the team by manager Jack Charlton.

CAPS

In his playing days, Brady goes down as having a total of 72 caps for Ireland's national football team.

MANAGEMENT CAREER

After fame filled career on the pitch, the Irish former footballer served as the Republic of Ireland national football team's assistant manager from 2008 to 2010.

Brady went on to manage two teams, Celtic and later Brighton & Hove Albion. And from 1996-2013, he was the Head of Youth Development at Arsenal, and he has been a regular television analyst for RTÉ Sport.

Chapter Twelve - ATHLETES

PART 3 - NICHOLAS CHRISTOPHER MICHAEL "CHRISTY" RING - HURLER (1920-1979)

START & CAREER

A right-wing-forward Irish hurler for the Cork senior team. Ring, who was born in Cloyne, County Cork, excelled in hurling as a kid. He made his inter-county debut at the age of sixteen, joining the Cork minor squad before moving on to the junior side. In the 1939-1940 National Hurling League, he made his senior debut.

AWARDS & VICTORIES

Ring went on to win eight All-Ireland medals, nine Munster medals, and three National Hurling League medals for Cork over the next twenty-four years. Ring was a two-time All-Ireland runner-up and captained the side to three All-Ireland titles.

A RECORD 23 SEASONS

Ring was a member of the Munster interprovincial squad for a record

23 seasons, winning an unprecedented eighteen Railway Cup trophies. No other player has ever reached double figures in the competition's history. He won 13 champion medals with Glen Rovers at club level.

Chapter Twelve - ATHLETES

PART 4 - RORY MCILROY, GOLFER, MBE (B. 1989)

A Northern Ireland-born professional golfer who competes on both the European and PGA Tours. He is the former World No. 1 and has won four major championships.

MAJORS

Rory became the first European to win 3 majors with his triumph at the Open Championship in July and joined Jack Nicklaus and Tiger Woods as the only players to win three majors by the age of 25. He won his second PGA Championship 3 weeks later, giving him a total of 4 major titles.

ACHIEVEMENTS

When he was just 22 years old, he became the youngest player on the European Tour to earn €10 million in career earnings in 2011. He led the Official World Golf Ranking, being #1 for the most weeks in the year of any golfer, 22 of the 52 weeks.

Chapter Twelve - ATHLETES

PLAYER OF THE YEAR

For the third time, McIlroy was named PGA Tour Player of the Year in 2019. (2012, 2014)

MAKETABLE

In 2013 he was considered the 3rd most marketable athlete in the world, next to Neymar and Lionel Messi. in 2013, he signed a deal with Nike worth a rumored $100-$250 million.

COUNTY DOWN

McIlroy lived in County Down, around 20 minutes from Belfast, near the small village of Moneyreagh.

UNICEF

McIlroy is a UNICEF Ireland Ambassador who made his first trip to Haiti with the organization in summer 2011.

MANCHESTER FOOTBALL

McIlroy is a fan of Manchester United F.C.

OPEN, MISS

In 2015, he tore his ankle ligaments while playing football with friends, forcing him to miss the Open Championship.

Chapter Twelve - ATHLETES

RUGBY
Ulster Rugby is a favorite of McIlroy's.

MBE
In the 2012 New Year Honours, McIlroy was named a Member of the Order of the British Empire (MBE) for services to sport.

2017 EARNINGS
Rory was the 6th highest paid sportsman in the world in 2017, earning $50 million.

AMAZON PRIME SHOW
McIlroy made an appearance in an episode of Amazon Prime's "The Grand Tour" in 2018, competing against Paris Hilton in the show's 'Celebrity Face-Off' portion.

WIFE
Rory married former PGA employee Erica Stoll in 2017 at Ashford Castle in County Mayo. Their daughter Poppy was born in September 2020.

PART 5 - WILLIAM JOSEPH DUNLOP, OBE, MOTORCYCLIST (1895-1965)

ACHIEVEMENTS

Ballymoney native and former world champion motorcyclist. Motorcycle News named Dunlop the seventh greatest motorcycle icon of all time in 2005. Triple hat-tricks at the Isle of Man TT meeting (1985, 1988, and 2000), where he won a total of 26 races and set the fastest lap (123.87). Dunlop claimed the Ulster Grand Prix 24x during his career and won the TT Formula One World Championship for the seventh time in 1986.

MBE

In 1986, he received the MBE for services to sport, and in 1996, he received the OBE for humanitarian work with kids in Romanian orphanages, to which he gave clothing and food. On June 11th, 2014, the documentary "Road," based on the lives of Joey Dunlop and his brothers, was released in the United Kingdom. He's appeared in 2 other documentary films, "V Four Victory" (1983) and Joey - The Man Who Conquered the TT (2013).

SUPERSTITIOUS

He owned a tavern in Ballymoney and was extremely superstitious, always racing in a red T-shirt and yellow crash helmet.

HONOR

Dunlop was chosen Northern Ireland's greatest sports star by Belfast Telegraph readers in 2015.

Chapter Twelve - ATHLETES

BOATING ACCIDENT

In 1985 while traveling by boat to the Isle of Man for the TT races, the former fishing boat Tornamora hit St. Patrick Rock, broke the rudder, and sank. All 13 passengers survived. The bikes were recovered later by divers.

SUPERSTITIOUS

He owned a tavern in Ballymoney and was extremely superstitious, always racing in a red T-shirt and yellow crash helmet.

ACCIDENT

Dunlop perished in Tallinn, Estonia, in 2000 after losing control of his motorcycle while leading a 125cc race.

FUNERAL

The funeral procession and ceremony at Garryduff Presbyterian church drew 50,000 mourners, including bikers from all across the United Kingdom and Ireland, as well as people from all walks of life in Northern Ireland.

JOEY DUNLOP CUP

The "Joey Dunlop Cup" is awarded to the overall winner of the yearly TT races. In his hometown of Ballymoney, a commemorative statue was erected in his honor.

STATUE

A statue of Dunlop sat atop a Honda stands guard over the Bungalow Bend in Snaefell on the Isle of Man.

Chapter Twelve - ATHLETES

PART 6 - PETER CANAVAN - GAELIC FOOTBALLER & MANAGER (B. 1971)

ACHIEVEMENTS

Among the most highly decorated players in the history of inter-county football, having won 2 All-Ireland Senior Championship medals, 6 All-Stars Awards, 4 provincial titles, two National Leagues, and numerous under-age & club championship medals. From 1998 to 2000, Canavan joined Ireland in the International Rules Series on multiple occasions. Pundits such as John Haughey of the BBC believe him to be one of the greatest players of the last two decades. He was named to the Sunday Tribune's "125 Most Influential People In GAA History" in 2009.

218 POINTS

His 218 points are the second-highest total in the Ulster Senior Football Championship's history.

DOES IT ALL

1995 Senior Football Championship, scored 11 of the team's 12 points and was described as a "one-man-show."

STATURE

Stands 1.73m tall (5ft-8in)

AKA

Nicknames are Peter "The Great" and "Petrol Pete"

Chapter Twelve - ATHLETES

TEAM
Played for Errigal Ciaran GAC 1990-2007

OCCUPATION
Physical Education Teacher at Holy Trinity College, Cookstown

FAMILY
He was born the 10th of 11 children

BROTHER
His older brother Pascal played on Tyrone with him in the 1990s

BREATHING
Suffers from asthma since childhood

TV CAREER
Is and has been a pundit and analyst for TV3, BBC, and Sky Sports

PART 7 - ALEX HIGGINS - SNOOKER (1949 - 2010)

ACHIEVEMENTS

Higgins earned World Champion status in 1972 & 1982, and runner-up in 1976 & again in 1980. He was dubbed Hurricane Higgins because of his quick play. One of only nine players to have achieved snooker's Triple Crown, he captured the UK Championship in 1983, as well as the Masters in 1978 & 1981. In 1984, he won the World Doubles title with Jimmy White, and in the same year with the All-Ireland team, won the World Cup three times.

POPULARITY

Known as the "People's Champion" and is frequently credited with introducing snooker to a larger public, Higgin's helped the game's popularity peak in the 1980s. He was known as a volatile and temperamental character.

VICES

He smoked heavily, suffered from alcohol and gambling addiction, and admitted to indulging in cocaine and marijuana. In 1998, Higgins was stricken with throat cancer and died from the disease in 2010 in his Belfast home.

Chapter Twelve - ATHLETES

SNOOKER START
Began playing snooker at 11 years old. At 14, was pursuing a career as a jockey but became too heavy

EARLY PLAY
Compiled his first maximum break (highest possible break in a single frame - 120 points) by age 16

Youngest to win the Northern Ireland amateurs at age 18. Turned professional at age 22

ABUSE OF OFFICIALS & OPPONENTS
Head butted an official during the UK Championship tournament in 1986

Punched official Colin Randle at the 1990 World Championship after losing in the first round to Steve James

Threatened to have fellow compatriot Dennis Taylor shot while they competed at the World Cup

TOBACCO HABIT
Reportedly smoked 80 cigarettes every day

FUNERAL
Fellow snooker pro Ken Doherty and Jimmy White were pallbearers at Higgins funeral held at St. Anne's Cathedral, Belfast, in 2010.

Chapter Twelve - ATHLETES

PART 8 - BRIAN O'DRISCOLL, RUGBY (B. 1979)

WHO IS BOD?

O'Driscoll is perhaps the most well-rounded, complete union player to wear a green jersey, following in the footsteps of Irish rugby greats such as Keith Wood, Simon Geoghegan, and Ollie Campbell. The Lions center was built to dominate with the oval ball in his hands and is also gifted with a sharp football intellect. O'Driscoll has won 3 Heineken Cups with hometown Leinster, in addition to his 4 Triple Crowns and single Grand Slam.

CAPTAIN

The Dublin-born player was an outside center for Ireland and the Irish regional team Leinster. From 2003 to 2012, he captained Ireland, as well as the British and Irish Lions during their New Zealand in 2005.

Critics consider him one of the finest rugby players in history.

ACHIEVEMENTS

O'Driscoll has 141 caps, 133 for Ireland (83 as captain) and 8 for the Lions, making him the fourth-most capped player in rugby union history. In 2001, he recorded 46 tries for Ireland, and then one for the Lions, making him the all-time leading try-scorer in Irish rugby. He is the eighth-highest try scorer in rugby union history and the all-time leading try-scorer in the center position.

HALL OF FAME
On November 17, 2016, he was admitted into the World Rugby Hall of Fame.

WORLD CUP
Part of Ireland's unsuccessful attempt to host the World Cup in 2023.

TV CAREER
Presently serves as a rugby pundit for BT Sport and ITV Sport.

BUSINESSMAN
A representative for the e-scooter start-up Zipp

RUGBY RUNS IN THE FAMILY
His father Frank played 2 games for Ireland, and Barry, a cousin of his dad, won 4 caps. Another

cousin of his dad's and Barry's brother named John represented Ireland 26 times.

FIRST LOVE WAS FOOTBALL
Brian originally played and excelled at Gaelic Football before transitioning to rugby.

Chapter Twelve - ATHLETES

U-19
Part of the 1998 Under 19 (U-19) Rugby World Champions team.

UNIVERSITY
Attended UCD under a full scholarship, graduating with a diploma in sports management

PLAYER OF THE YEAR, ACCOLADES
Was nominated for IRB World Player of the Year in 2001, 2002 & 2009.RBS Six Nations Championships was chosen as the 2006, 2007 & 2009 Player of the Tournament

Rugby World Magazine voted Brian the World Rugby Player of the Decade (2000's)

HONORARY RECOGNITION
Owns 3 honorary doctorates, 1 each from Dublin City university, Queens University Belfast & Trinity College Dublin.

WIFE
He is married to Actress Amy Huberman, known as "Daisy" in the drama series "The Clinic" on RTE. They have three children together: Sadie, Billy, and Ted.

ROYALTY
Both Brian and wife Amy were invited to Prince William's and Catherine Middleton's wedding. Brian did not attend due to Leinster's Heineken Cup semi-final game the next day.

MANCHESTER
He is a fan of the football club Manchester United F.C.

PART 9 - ROBERT (ROBBIE) KEANE - FORMER FOOTBALL FORWARD (B. 1980)

CAPTAIN

Tallaght, Dublin-born Robbie Keane, a former forward and the captain of the Republic of Ireland from 2006 to 2016. Keane has the most caps and is the team's all-time leading goal-scorer. He was recently Middlesbrough's assistant manager.

ACHIEVEMENTS

Keane scored 65 goals for the Irish national team, earning him the all-time leading scorer in the country. Behind Hungary's Puskás and Kocsis and Germany's Gerd Müller and Klose, he was at one time the sixth highest-scoring European in history. Keane was Ireland's leading top goal-scorer at the 2002 World Cup, scoring three goals in the country's run to the quarterfinals while also having represented Ireland at UEFA Euro 2012.

COACHING

In November 2018, Keane started his coaching career with the Ireland senior squad under Mick McCarthy's management structure after announcing his retirement from playing. In 2019, he also played the role of assistant manager at Middlesbrough in the Championship, where his former colleague Jonathan Woodgate is the manager. Keane signed a one-year deal with Middlesbrough, which expired in June 2020, and he departed the club on his own terms. Keane worked towards his UEFA Pro Licence while working at both jobs, earning his license in 2020.

Chapter Twelve - ATHLETES

PERSONAL STATS
Born July 8th, 1980. He is 1.75 m tall (5 foot 9 inches)

FORMER GAELIC FOOTBALL PLAYER
Played Gaelic Football until the age of 15. Quitting to focus on Football (soccer)

MLS TENURE
Joined the MLS LA Galaxy in 20011, playing alongside David Beckham and Landon Donovan.

CELEBRATION
Keane's characteristic goal-scoring celebration consisted of him doing a cartwheel, a forward roll, and then getting up and simulating the shooting of pistols with his hands.

WIFE
Keane married former Miss Ireland contestant Claudine Palmer in Ballybrack on 7 June 2008. They have 2 sons, Robert and Hudson.

FAMOUS COUSIN
Keane can count famous English singer Morrisey as a cousin.

FAMOUS COUSIN #2
2nd highest goal-scorer in League Ireland history, Jason Byrne, is a first cousin.

U.S. GREEN CARD
Holds a U.S. green card, mostly for MLS play - pay - residency qualification.

PART 10 - CONOR MCGREGOR - 3 WEIGHT CLASS MMA FIGHTER AND BOXER (B. 1988)

The "Notorious" Conor (Anthony) McGregor. Arguably the most popular athlete in Ireland's long history of sport. But there would be zero arguments with McGregor's status as the #1 draw for the UFC, the world's largest and most profitable fighting

organization. To date, Conor has been credited with headlining 5 of the 6 largest Pay-Per-Views in UFC (and MMA) History, including 2.4M buys for UFC 229.

CHAMP-CHAMP

At one time, McGregor simultaneously held the promotions 145lb and 155lb divisions championship belts, a feat he had also achieved just a few years earlier in the smaller organization known as Cage Warriors.

3-WEIGHT CLASS SUCCESS

The former 145lb featherweight and 155lb lightweight champion has also competed successfully at the 170lb Welterweight Division.

BOXING WITH FLOYD MAYWEATHER JR.

But perhaps the Crumlin born (southside suburb of Dublin) is most recognized for the famous MMA vs. Boxing match vs. the undefeated Floyd Mayweather Jr. Although McGregor came up short, he gained a lot of respect from fans worldwide and gave Mayweather a decent challenge for their 4.3M PPV buys event.

TRASH-TALKER

Along with his fighting skills, McGregor was revolutionary in MMA trash-talk and garnered fans not only in Ireland but worldwide. Conor's quick wit and fight selling vernacular is said to be on par with boxing legend Muhammad Ali.

PREDICTIONS

Besides (The) "Notorious" nickname, Conor has also dubbed himself "Mystic Mac" for his uncanny ability to predict his fight's outcomes with surprising accuracy, both results, round #'s, and how he'll finish. Is he a swami or incredibly talented and astute at studying his opponents?

#1 $$$$$

Because of his popular fighting style, quick wit, and never-fear attitude, McGregor was named the 4th highest-paid athlete in 2018, making $99 million. In 2021 at the age of 33, he was named Forbes' #1 highest-paid athlete after making a whopping $180 million.

Chapter Twelve - ATHLETES

RECENT LOSSES

Although his record has added numerous high-profile losses as of late, all of these come at the highest level of the sport vs. current and former champions and also multi-time title contenders.

"MONEY-FIGHT" ERA

He continues to be a massive draw within the sport and UFC promotion, making him the top of the list fighter call-outs - Other fighters time on the Mic after a win, daring Conor for battle in the ever-popular "Money-fight" era.

170LB RUN RUMORS

Conor has been sidelined for some time after suffering an in-ring brutal leg break in a fight with long-time rival Dustin "The Diamond" Poirier. He is expected to return in 2022 and has since put on a lot of mass and strength with rumors of a run at the 170 welter-weight crown. If successful, he will become the only man in MMA and UFC history to win a title in the same organization in 3 different weight classes.

MMA STYLE

MMA Style is officially listed as "Boxing."

LEFTY

Conor's default fight positioning is a south-paw (left-handed) wide-legged karate stance, though often switches to orthodox (right-handed) for striking advantages.

Chapter Twelve - ATHLETES

JIU-JITSU CREDENTIALS
He is a Jiu-Jitsu Brown Belt under (coach) John Kavanagh

MMA WINS
He has 22 wins: 19 by knockout, 1 by submission, 2 by decision

MMA LOSSES
He has 6 losses: 2 by knockout, 4 by submission

FIRST SPORT
He played football (soccer) in his youth and dreamed one day of playing professionally.

FOOTBALL SUPPORT
He supports Celtic and Manchester United, and his friend Sergio Ramos' Paris Saint-Germain.

PRE MMA CAREER
Was an apprentice plumber before becoming a full-time MMA fighter

FIRST FIGHT
Made his amateur debut on February 17th, 2007, vs. Kieran Campbell for the Irish Ring of Truth promotion. He won via TKO in the very first round

1ST UFC IRISHMAN
2013 he was just the 2nd ever Irish fighter signed to the UFC (1st = Tom Egan)

Chapter Twelve - ATHLETES

1ST IRISHMAN TO BE UFC CHAMPION
Was the first-ever Irishman - world champion of the UFC, winning the 145lb Featherweight Interim championship in January of 2015 and the unified belt in August 2015

FIRST LOSS
Conor's 1st loss came at the hands of UFC's Ultimate Fighter Season 5 winner Nate Diaz in 2016.

HERO
Conor admires and emulates fellow karate stylist Bruce Lee

FIANCÉ
Conor has been with his fiancé Dee Devlin since 2008. They have 3 children: Rian, Croatia, and Conor Jr.

SPONSORSHIPS
Has corporate sponsorships with Burger King, Bud Light, Reebok, Beats by Dre, and Monster Energy Drink

WHISKEY BRAND
Launched "Proper No. Twelve Irish Whiskey" in late 2018

BREAKING THE LAW

Has had run-ins with the law several times including, speeding, traffic violation, and arrests for robbery, multiple assaults, and suspicion of sexual assault. The charges ended in fines, dropped charges, and probations; no serious-lengthy incarceration time.

PART 11 - RANDOM FAST FACTS #8

MARRIAGES
In 2018, there were 20,389 male-female marriages.

NO GIRLS
Female Leprechauns do not exist. Only male Leprechauns are depicted in all artwork and legends.

LIMERICK
Limerick is a county in Ireland but is also found in 10 different places around the world: 8 in the U.S., 1 in Ireland, and 1 in Saskatchewan, Canada.

VISION
According to a Bayer survey, 56 percent of Irish adults wear glasses. A further 8% elect to wear contact lenses = 2/3 of the Irish people need corrective lenses.

BOOK OF KELLS
The 8th century "Book of Kells" residing in Dublin's Trinity University was written in Latin.

COASTAL ROAD
The Wild Atlantic Way is the world's longest coastal driving road, 2,600 km or 1,600 miles.

Chapter Twelve - ATHLETES

BUENOS AIRES PARADE
The largest St. Patrick's Day celebration in South America takes place in Buenos Aires, Argentina.

TOUR DE FRANCE
13-year pro cyclist Stephen Roche of Ireland won the 1987 Tour de France.

SOAP OPERA
RTÉ's (Radio TV Ireland) began broadcasting soap opera "Fair City" back in 1989, 33 years and running.

OBAMA
Barack Obama's Irish ancestors can be traced to County Offaly, Leinster.

SIGN LANGUAGE
Due to historically segregated education, men and women utilize different hand signals in Irish Sign Language.

CENTENARIAN CELEBRATION
Ireland's Centenarian Bounty is a letter and €2,540 from the President on your 100th birthday. Folks get a letter and a souvenir coin on each successive birthday.

NOBEL & OSCAR
George Bernard Shaw, an Irish writer, is the first individual to win both a Nobel Prize and an Academy Award; Oscar for best-written screenplay and a Nobel Prize for literature.

Chapter Twelve - ATHLETES

PART 12 - CREDITS

ILLUSTRATIONS

Each and every Illustration(s) are paid for and fully licensed with permission for commercial use from copyright holder - artist Ron Leishman and toonaday.com

Information sources

gov.ie

citezensinformation.ie

britannica.com

fullbrightscholarship.net

travel.state.gov (ireland)

ireland-information.com

nationsonline.org

foreign.com

tradingeconomics.com

howtopronounce.com

dictionary.cambridge.org

mentalfloss.com

wikipedia.com

youtube

swedishnomad.com

irishtimes.com

irelandbeforeyoudie.com

unbelievable-facts.com

Chapter Twelve - ATHLETES

Todayifoundout.com

irisharoundtheworld.com

worldstrides.com

listchallenges.com

unbelievablefactsblog.com

jetpunk.com

funtrivia.com

theirishroadtrip.com

eupedia.com

globeexperiences.com

skyscanner.ie

theworldpursuit.com

gotoquiz.com

baltimoremagazine.com

irishamerica.com

bostonirish.com

trustedtours.com

toughtco.com

anewcare.com

chicagotribune.com

bostonglobe.com

neworleans.com

eatdrinktravel.com

ireland-information.com

meanwhileinireland.com

climatestotravel.com

weatherspark.com

Chapter Twelve - ATHLETES

vagabondtoursofireland.com

worthly.com

irishamericanmom.com

irish-genealogy-toolkit.com

irishpost.com

mappr.co

ireland.com

everyculture.com

emerald-heritage.com

abc57.com

aoh.com

dailyorange.com

thespruceeats.com

justfunfacts.com

tripsavvy.com

wildernessireland.com

CONGRATULATIONS
YOU FINISHED

 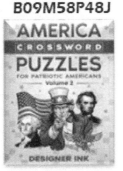  

Made in United States
Orlando, FL
24 March 2022

16105824R00122